The Feasts Of The Kingdom

Sermons On Holy Communion
And Other Sacred Meals

Maurice A. Fetty

CSS Publishing Company, Inc., Lima, Ohio

THE FEASTS OF THE KINGDOM

Copyright © 2002 by
CSS Publishing Company, Inc.
Lima, Ohio

All rights reserved. No part of this publication may be reproduced in any manner whatsoever without the prior permission of the publisher, except in the case of brief quotations embodied in critical articles and reviews. Inquiries should be addressed to: Permissions, CSS Publishing Company, Inc., P.O. Box 4503, Lima, Ohio 45802-4503.

Unless marked otherwise, scripture quotations are from the *New Revised Standard Version of the Bible*, copyright 1989 by the Division of Christian Education of the National Council of the Churches of Christ in the USA. Used by permission.

Scripture quotations marked (KJV) are from the *King James Version of the Bible*, in the public domain.

Scripture quotations marked (NEB) are from *The New English Bible*. Copyright © the Delegates of the Oxford University Press and the Syndics of the Cambridge University Press, 1961, 1970. Reprinted by permission.

Scripture quotations marked (RSV) are from the *Revised Standard Version of the Bible*, copyrighted 1946, 1952 ©, 1971, 1973, by the Division of Christian Education of the National Council of the Churches of Christ in the USA. Used by permission.

For more information about CSS Publishing Company resources, visit our website at www.csspub.com or e-mail us at custserv@csspub.com or call (800) 241-4056.

ISBN 0-7880-1941-4   PRINTED IN U.S.A.

Dedicated to

the loving memory

of

my mother

Eva Carol Smith Fetty
(1906-1992)

and my father

Clifford Allen Fetty
(1906-1987)

For my mother, food was love and love was food. Meals were family occasions around the kitchen or dining room table. They were sacramental times — times for saying grace, telling stories, laughing, sharing, and of course, helping with the dishes.

They were "feasts of the kingdom," sacred meals, food for body and soul, reflections of Holy Communion, over which my father, as an Elder of the church, helped preside.

Table Of Contents

Preface   7

Advent

1. A Feast For The Faithful   9
   Isaiah 40:11

2. Waiting At The Table   15
   1 Corinthians 11:26

3. Life, Light, And Enlightenment   21
   John 1:4-5

Lent

4. Bread For The Journey   29
   Exodus 16:11-12

5. What Will You Have — Dancing Or Fasting?   37
   Matthew 11:17

6. Faith And Fast-Food Religion   45
   John 6:67-68

7. Parties, Perfumes, And The Poor   51
   John 12:7-8

8. The Dinner Party Not To Miss   61
   Luke 14:23-24

9. Parable Of The Marriage Feast   71
   Matthew 22:14

10. The Great Invitation   81
    Matthew 22:14

Palm/Passion Sunday

11. The Hunger Pangs Of Success   89
    Philippians 2:5-7

Easter

12.	Dinner At Emmaus *Luke 24:30-31, 35*	99
13.	Breakfast On The Beach *John 21:9, 12*	109
14.	The Ultimate Wedding Reception *Revelation 19:9*	117

Pentecost

15.	Sacraments For Sometimes Secular People *Matthew 28:19-20*	127
16.	Eating And Drinking Toward Spiritual Health *1 Corinthians 11:29-30*	139
17.	The Bread Of Life *John 6:35*	147
18.	Water And The Thirst For Life *Psalm 63:1*	155
19.	Thirst — And The Living Waters *John 4:13-14*	163
20.	Dinner With A Jealous Brother *Luke 15:29*	171
21.	Communion And Companionship *1 Corinthians 10:17*	181
22.	Chicken Soup And Other Remedies *Philippians 4:8*	189
23.	The Yeast Of The Pharisees And Herod *Mark 8:15*	199
24.	A Spiritual Bouquet For A Spiritual Banquet *Galatians 5:22-23*	205
25.	Table Manners In A Hungry World *Luke 16:20-21*	213
26.	The Feast Of Expectation *Revelation 7:16-17*	221

Bibliography	227

Preface

Feasts and festivals have been central to many religions of the world. This has been true especially of Judaism and Christianity. For Judaism, the Passover was, and is, central. And for Christianity, Communion or the Eucharist or the Lord's Supper or the Mass, as it is variously called, is central. In many Christian churches, Holy Communion is celebrated weekly. In others it is observed monthly or on a quarterly basis.

Holy Communion is, for Christians, the new "Passover Feast," commemorating the sacrificial death of Jesus, the "Paschal Lamb" of the New Covenant. By his death and resurrection, Christians believe people are, like the ancient Hebrews, liberated from bondage and death. The "death angel" passes over them. Thus, on the night before his death, Jesus instituted the Eucharist or Holy Communion in his Last Supper with his disciples. It was to become a feast of memory, celebration, and presence. Because of his death, the "death angel" would "pass over" the disciples.

Early Christians may have first celebrated Communion in their "Love Feasts," wherein the bread and wine of the common fellowship meal were blessed in memory of Jesus. Eventually separated from "Love Feasts" and placed in the center of Christian worship, the bread and wine became elements of a spiritual feast. They were the "food of immortality," by which the soul was strengthened for its earthly pilgrimage and assured of life everlasting.

In our common acts of eating and drinking, sustenance for body and soul are given, and a sense of community is developed. In a sometimes lonely world, we are assured we are not alone. Nurtured with the bounty of earth, we also are nurtured by the love and laughter of those sharing with us.

Likewise in the spiritual feast at the heart of the Church's worship. We share in the elements of the earth, but even more, share in the spiritual realities of forgiveness and acceptance, grace and encouragement, as well as the joy and reassurance of the Divine Presence.

Therefore, in all our eating and drinking we demonstrate our dependence upon Divine providence and grace, while at the same time celebrating the joys of food and drink and the promises of fellowship now and in the life everlasting.

1. A Feast For The Faithful

He will feed his flock like a shepherd, he will gather the lambs in his arms, he will carry them in his bosom, and gently lead those that are with young.
— Isaiah 40:11

Our Advent text today from Isaiah 40 dates from a time when ancient Iraq, known as Babylonia, was in the news. The beautiful text, written in 550 B.C., by an unknown prophet we call the Second Isaiah, was first preached to Jewish exiles in Babylonia (now Iraq) on the shores of the Euphrates River (or by a canal) in Babylon, the fabled capital city.

A few years earlier, in 587 B.C., King Nebuchadnezzar of Babylonia had conquered Judah, destroyed the capital city of Jerusalem as well as Solomon's beautiful Temple, and had carried the Jewish nobility into exile to Babylonia. Nebuchadnezzar regarded himself a world conqueror and named himself king of kings.

Ironically, in our time, Saddam Hussein of Iraq has seen himself as Nebuchadnezzar's successor. Until recently Hussein was excavating and restoring ancient Babylon and Babylon's famous hanging gardens. Hussein had believed that under his leadership and military prowess, the boundaries of Iraq would expand to those of ancient Babylonia, to include not only Iraq, but also Kuwait, Syria, Jordan, and Lebanon with Israel under Babylonian or Iraqi control as it was in Isaiah's time.

Defying usual archeological norms, Hussein ordered replicas of the ancient buildings erected on the original sites. He offered a $1.5 million reward for anyone who could develop a satisfactory plan to restore the hanging gardens, now a pile of brick and dirt. In tourist pamphlets, Nebuchadnezzar is celebrated for his dual roles as civilian and military leader, for his recovery of lost lands, and for his love of great buildings.

When the reporter asked a leading archeologist if Iraqis considered Hussein the new Nebuchadnezzar, she laughed and answered,

"Yes, of course" (*New York Times*, October 11, 1990, A13). Then the archeologist added: "History repeats itself." Referring to the time Isaiah wrote and preached his famous sermon, she said, "The Persians and the Jewish, they wanted to destroy us then, and they are still trying to destroy us now" (*ibid.*). Except, of course, Hussein is the present aggressor.

As a matter of fact, shortly after Isaiah preached his message of hope to his fellow Jewish exiles, Cyrus the Persian defeated the Babylonians and changed the balance of power once again in the Near East. Isaiah, in a later sermon, even names Cyrus as God's messiah, his agent to liberate the Jews to allow them to return to their homeland.

Saddam Hussein, the modern Nebuchadnezzar, had conquest and domination on his mind. He lusted after power and longed to be the leader of the Arab world, the king of kings. Consequently, in Advent, Isaiah's words have a new ironic relevance. God will come to his people, says Isaiah. Have faith.

I.

Isaiah reminds us that *God comes to us through nature, through the natural world.*

After some years in Babylonia, the Jewish exiles began to wonder if God had forgotten them. The Babylonians were so powerful. Their cities were splendid, abounding in architectural masterpieces. Babylonian culture was rather high and sophisticated and Babylonian religion was colorful and intricate.

Consequently, uprooted from their familiar terrain and having undergone culture shock, the Jewish exiles wondered if God had forgotten them, or whether he even cared at all.

It was then Isaiah, speaking by the inspiration of God's Spirit, urged the exiles to look up into the brilliant Babylonian nighttime sky. Look at all the stars, the hosts of heaven. Can you count them? Of course not. And yet God not only counts them, he knows them by name. It is God, and not the Babylonian deity, Marduk, who has created all these. God comes to us through the faithfulness of the natural world, said Isaiah.

Urban dwellers that we are, removed in distance and psychology from the agrarian and natural world, we have to be reminded of the sacramental aspects of all the natural world. Preoccupied as we are with machines, money, and technology, we easily can ignore our dependence upon the faithfulness of the seasons and seedtime and harvest. Predisposed toward our own concerns and activities, we frequently overlook the faithful activities of millions of life forms so that we can survive.

Appropriately then, our Communion Feast is one with real bread and real wine. Rather than a mystical experience of abstract thought and reverie, our Communion is real eating and drinking of real bread and wine. All the world and its produce are signs of God's faithful coming to us. In his providential love and care, God provides abundantly all our necessary food and drink.

Therefore, with Isaiah, we celebrate God's faithful coming to us in the produce of the earth and in the faithfulness of the natural world.

II.

If we celebrate God's coming to us in the natural world, in Advent we celebrate even more *God's coming to us in the world of human nature, in human history.*

Few Americans have experienced what the ancient Jewish exiles experienced. We have not known the devastation of war on our soil since the Civil War, or the "War Between the States." While thousands of our soldiers have died in foreign lands, few of our civilians have been exiled by a foreign power. The structures of our government, economy, and religion have not been overthrown by an alien power. The Stars and Stripes have flown uninterrupted over our Capitol for years.

For the Jews, 587 years before Christ, it was different. The Babylonians had looted and destroyed their cities. Women were raped, homes and goods pillaged and confiscated. The leading families, priests, politicians, and military people were captured and taken to an alien land.

Later the Jewish exiles wrote a song about their experience which has been included in our Bible. In ancient Iraq they sang,

> *By the waters of Babylon,*
> *there we sat down and wept,*
> *when we remembered Zion (Jerusalem).*
>
> *On the willows there*
> *we hung up our lyres.*
> *For there our captors*
> *required of us songs,*
> *and our tormentors, mirth, saying,*
> *"Sing us one of the songs of Zion!"*
> *How shall we sing the Lord's song*
> *in a foreign land?* — Psalm 137:1-4

Isaiah's answer was not a subjective one. He did not suggest that the exiles whip themselves into an emotional frenzy to forget their captivity or to produce false hopes. Nor did he assume a fatalistic philosophy of history suggesting that what is, is, and that there is nothing you can do about it. Nor did he advise cynicism or materialistic pragmatism or a skeptical resignation to hopelessness.

Instead, Isaiah urged them to look at what was happening in world politics. He called their attention to the fact that King Nebuchadnezzar, the so-called king of kings, had died in 562 B.C. He urged them to pay attention to Cyrus, from the small province of Elam — Cyrus who overcame the Assyrians and Medes and gained control of the Persian Empire. God is calling Cyrus, said Isaiah, to be his anointed one, his Messiah, to change the course of history.

And Isaiah was right, for in 539 B.C., Cyrus defeated the Babylonians, and granted freedom to the Jewish exiles to return to their homeland. God is faithful not only to provide for us in the natural world, says Isaiah. He also is faithful in the human natural world, the world of human history.

For Christians, God's faithfulness to human history is borne out in the coming of God's own Son into history itself. Rather than leaving the human race in exile as on a forgotten planet, God has, in the words of J. B. Phillips, made the world the "visited planet," the place of God's special, liberating activity. Not only does God sustain us physically, he also nurtures us spiritually and morally, not by what *we* do, but by what *he* does.

Therefore, as we gather at the feast for the faithful, the focus is on what *God* does, not on what *we* do. As theologian Donald Baillie put it, "... we ... approach the Lord's table not looking inwards upon our own souls and striving to work up an effect in the realm of feeling and emotion, but looking beyond ourselves to him who is waiting to be gracious to us...." (*Theology of the Sacraments*, p. 107).

In this time of history when King Nebuchadnezzar's successors have again threatened world peace, we gather at the feast for the faithful to be reminded that God is the King of Kings; and that it is God who has come to us in the past, and who will come to us in the future to make our lives whole and complete. We are reminded by Isaiah that nations are no more than a drop in a bucket. Political leaders come and go, rise and fall. We are reminded that all flesh is grass, as the flower of the field, which today is and then withers.

We come to the feast for the faithful to be reminded we belong most of all to God's eternal kingdom. God will not disappoint us. Have faith, says Isaiah. God will care for his own.

Prayer

Almighty God, Creator of the Milky Way, Mars, and the Moon, who scatters galaxies throughout the universe and places solar systems in orbit, you are awesome in power and glorious in your majesty. Frail and temporal as we are, we can only praise your greatness and kneel in the presence of your power.

And yet you have spoken to us not only in power, but in love. You have manifested yourself not only in judgment, but in mercy. Giver of the laws of humanity and the natural order, you approach us not only with the severity of a judge, but the compassion of a counselor. Never abandoning us to the harshness and cruelty of an uncaring world, you desire to lead us as a gentle shepherd and to gather us up in your arms of love.

Speak tenderly to us today, O Lord God, Father of us all. Look out among us to behold the broken hearts, the bruised souls, the torn and fractured relationships, the disappointments and rejections, the heartache and despair, and all the agony which is to be found in our human loving. Take all wounded souls into your loving arms and nourish them and restore them to health and confidence.

And for those of us grown cynical and blasé; for those of us smug in our self-conceits and content in our complacency; for those of us mired in skepticism and arrested in unbelief; for those of us snickering in our snobbery, arrogant not only before our fellowman, but even before you, believing that you are to be our servile, heavenly servant; for these and all our prideful pretensions, forgive us, O Lord, and come to us with the judgment we deserve and the forgiveness we desperately need.

Hear us as we pray for the nations of the world. Grant wisdom, courage, and strength to all world leaders. Grant that peace might prevail over war and bloodshed, O Lord. In Christ's name we pray. Amen.

2. Waiting At The Table

For as often as you eat this bread and drink this cup, you proclaim the Lord's death until he comes.
— 1 Corinthians 11:26

It may not have occurred to you this morning as you ate your Kellogg's Corn Flakes that you were biting into a segment of religious history somewhat related to the season of Advent. Dr. John H. Kellogg of cereal fame, in Battle Creek, Michigan, became a protégé of Ellen White, a prominent member of the Adventist group which began to flourish in this country in the mid-nineteenth century. Dr. Kellogg, convinced vegetarian, was devoted to making varieties of foods from cereal grains so as to avoid eating animal flesh.

But vegetarians and corn flakes were a minor part of something more important in American religious history. White and Kellogg were followers of an unusual Baptist minister, William Miller, who conducted revival meetings in Vermont, New Hampshire, and New York. Miller had spent years studying the prophecies of the Bible, especially Daniel, regarding the end of time.

He began to give lectures and preach sermons announcing the Second Coming of Christ would be soon and that the end of the world was close at hand. He lectured all across the country between 1840 and 1843, over 300 times in just a half a year. Thousands flocked to hear him. Miller advised people to prepare themselves for the Lord's Second Coming, his triumphal Advent.

William Miller began to be more specific. The Second Coming, he announced, would take place in March, 1843. There were heavenly signs, even a comet, which seemed to signal Christ's imminent return. The date came and went, and was reset for March, 1844. People quit their jobs and waited in expectation. Yet another date was set, this time October 22, 1844, for the Lord's return. In upstate New York people again quit their jobs and waited on the hilltops. And while the Second Coming never materialized, out of that expectation the Seventh Day Adventist Church did materialize and out of them the Jehovah's Witnesses.

Miller and others capitalized on the sentiment of expectation and waiting that is explicit in the biblical religions of Judaism and Christianity. If some religions of the world, notably some of the Eastern, have a cyclical view of history, Judaism and Christianity have a linear view. For them, history is going somewhere. It has a beginning and it has an end. It is limited and finite, coming into being in time and space, only to be absorbed into a final consummation.

And now that the new millennium is with us, we will hear a great deal more about the expected end of the world and the Second Coming of Christ. Christians, expecting a millennium, a thousand-year reign of Christ upon the earth, were excited when the year 1000 approached. Many quit their jobs and made sure their souls were pure to meet the triumphant Christ as he descended from heaven. And now in this new millennium, we may expect similar kinds of activity. (Work to keep your hearts pure, but before you quit your job, let's talk!)

While we may smile at the somewhat naive expectancy of many, we do well to remember that at the heart of our faith is the anticipation of the Lord's Advent, his coming again into history. The Christian Church has often thought of itself as a waiting community, a community of faith waiting for the consummation of history and the *apokatastasis*, the restoration of all things.

That is why Paul reminded them that while they were together at the Communion table, sharing the bread and wine, they were "proclaiming the Lord's death until he comes again." As a consequence, Christians have been waiting at the table ever since; waiting for the final resolution of history as we know it; waiting for the full messianic age; waiting for the life everlasting.

Thus in this Advent Season, waiting as we are around the Communion Table, we are advised to do at least two things: be patient and be expectant.

I.

Consider first this matter of *patience*.

The Church has struggled with this matter of patience from the very beginning. The first generation of Christians believed the Second Coming of Christ and the end of the world would take place in their lifetime. That is one reason they took so long to write down their Sacred Scriptures. With history coming to an end soon, they reasoned they wouldn't need any historical writings. Nor would they need to give careful attention to creeds and liturgies and organizational questions. They were a provisional community of faith, waiting at the table for the end.

Peter's second letter addresses the problem of the delayed Second Coming. Some Christians had begun to give up their Christian morality, claiming it didn't matter anymore, since the Second Coming wasn't going to happen. Greed and licentiousness began to infect some. Others returned to old myths and fables as a source of consolation. Others delighted in being resident skeptics and cynics.

But Peter advises them, "Do not ignore this one fact, beloved, that with the Lord one day is as a thousand years, and a thousand years as one day" (2 Peter 3:8). He then warns them God is not slow about his promises, but is teaching us patience and giving us the opportunity for repentance. For the Lord will come, says Peter, like a thief in the night. Therefore, you ought to consider the kind of lives you should be living. And you should learn patience.

When you think of it, impatience is often a sign of greed. We want it all, and we want it *now*. So we become compulsively acquisitive, compulsively obsessive, determined to take all that we can from life and make it our own. So whether it be money or power, pleasure or fame, we grasp for it all now because we are impatient. We don't want to wait for it.

Impatience is then a sign of deeper malaise, an anxiety about life in general and our life in particular. Perpetually discontent with what we have, we become anxious over what we have not. Even in our prayers we ask and do not receive, "because," says James, "we ask wrongly, to spend it on our passions" (4:3).

Jesus warned us about undue anxiety in his famous Sermon on the Mount. Don't be obsessed with worry. Look at the birds of the air and the lilies of the fields. God provides for them, will he not also provide for you?

Patience is indeed a virtue. It reminds us that we do not control history. Nor can we manipulate God. Patience gives us time for the development of the inner man, the inner woman. It reminds us even at table that the kingdom of God is more than gourmet food and drink, but peace and joy in the Holy Spirit. Patience allows us to come to the spiritual maturity intended by God. It allows us time to grow out of the me, me, me stage, to put away childish and selfish ways of thinking and behaving, and to become radiant and serene with inner confidence and hope.

So while we are waiting at the table for the Lord's return, we should learn patience with ourselves, with each other and with God.

II.

Consider next the matter of *expectancy*.

Biblical scholar J. Harry Cotton once said history has an offspring in its womb the world cannot imagine. He knew, as most biblical scholars know, that there is more to come in this grand scheme of things entire. All the realities of the present are pregnant with the future. And the future depends to some degree on our expectancy, our readiness to receive the future.

Dr. Leander Keck of Yale University wrote a fine book recently, his Lyman Beecher Lectures, titled *The Church Confident*. In it he laments the rather lackadaisical nature of much mainline Protestant worship. In our self-centeredness, we have secularized worship, says Dr. Keck. "The worship of God," says Keck, "is useful in helping us make actual our ideal secular selves; mature, self-motivated, able to develop our full potential, urbane in outlook ... And above all feeling good about ourselves" (p. 34).

And for some, says Professor Keck, the Communion elements represent not Christ's passion, but "our creative powers." The Eucharist no longer celebrates the breaking of God's Son for us, but the potential for healing ourselves. So God is reduced to the Great Enabler whose sole purpose in the universe is to glorify us. And if the Westminster Confession used to ask and answer, "What is the chief end of man? The chief end of man is to glorify God and enjoy him forever," modern worshipers, says Keck, turn it around to say the "chief end of God is to glorify us and to be useful to us indefinitely" (pp. 34-36).

Consequently, with the sense of expectancy gone, God becomes an amiable bore and worship a memorial service to a fire gone out (*ibid.*, p. 36). Nothing happens in worship because we want it to happen on *our* terms. Nothing happens in worship because we expect nothing to happen. Preoccupied with ourselves, our agendas, our goals and purposes, we wait for a God who never comes as Beckett waited for Godot — a God who never comes because we have lost the sense of humble expectancy.

Reinhold Niebuhr taught at Union Theological Seminary for many years. He captured not only the eyes and ears of American religious leadership; he captured the eyes and ears and minds of many political leaders. In his classic two-volume work, *The Nature and Destiny of Man*, he contrasts those societies which expect a coming Messiah with those who don't.

Messiah-expectant societies had about them, said Niebuhr, an openness and sense of urgency. They tended to be future-oriented more than past-oriented. Hope prevailed over despair, and belief in progress prevailed over a sense of regression and futility.

As with cultures and societies so with individuals, when we expect a Messiah our minds and souls are turned upward toward infinity, rather than downward toward finiteness. When we expect a Messiah, we believe more in our future potential than our past failures. When we expect a Messiah we are more calm about success, knowing that all success is tentative and transient and will be swallowed up in God's larger development and consummation.

When we lose our sense of expectancy, when we lose the sense of anticipation and the dimension of hope and excitement, we begin to die. We start closing the pages on life and history and presume that since our faith and hope are coming to an end everything else is. Expectancy, on the other hand, keeps us alive and vibrant. As Dr. Cotton said, history has an offspring in its womb the world cannot imagine.

William Miller, the Baptist minister who inspired thousands, and Dr. John Kellogg of Kellogg's Corn Flakes, had their dates wrong, but many of their ideas were right. The Christian community should be a patient and expectant community, awaiting the Lord's Second Advent, not so much on a hilltop in upstate New York, as around a table, a Communion Table, wherever we are.

Christ's Second Coming may not occur in the year 2003, or even for another millennium or twenty. But the ending of our life and our coming to Christ may happen any time. And what better way to be prepared for either event than to be "waiting at the table."

Prayer

Eternal God, who out of the generative power of your Being has set the universe in motion, and who, by the revolutions and rotations of our solar system, has given us the sense of time, we bow in your presence, reverent with the realization of our transience and humbled by the knowledge of the limitations of all our powers. We are indeed sojourners upon the earth, pilgrims in passage through time and space, voyagers of faith and hope to destinations beyond space and time. And we sense you have begun it all, and in your good time will bring it all to an end.

So it is, Lord God, we are learning to wait, learning to be patient, learning your sense of timing, learning to perceive your scheme of things entire.

Be pleased then to assist us in our waiting. Some of us are waiting for our ship to come in, waiting for our stock to rise, waiting for our life-changing opportunity, waiting for our place in the sun. Others of us are waiting for the prodigal to come home, or the husband or wife to return, or the friend to forgive. Help us, O Lord, not to keep anyone waiting for the forgiveness we need to grant or the love we need to show.

Above all, as we await the Lord's Advent and the restoration of all things, help us to be patient and hopeful. Save us from the stuffiness of skepticism and the smugness of easy cynicism. Cause us to look to you, to be expectant and hopeful, radiant with the confidence that in your good time, you do all things well. Through Jesus Christ our Lord. Amen.

3. Life, Light, And Enlightenment

*In him was life, and the life was the light of men.
The light shines in the darkness, and the darkness
has not overcome it.* — John 1:4-5

Summer is the season of sun worshipers. In the Northern Hemisphere millions of sunbathers will make their way to the beaches to "soak up the rays." Northerners from winter-grey Scandinavia, Germany, Belgium, and France will press southward by every conveyance for the glistening beaches of the French, Spanish, and Italian Rivieras.

Russians will push toward the Baltic. Australians, in their wintertime, will forge northward to the Great Barrier Reef. And New Yorkers will migrate by millions to Long Island beaches and New England lakes to soak up the sun for that healthy summer look. Yes, despite warnings of skin cancer, sun worshipers by the millions will rub on sun screen and yield themselves again to the heavenly deity — El Sol, old Mister Sun.

If we worship the sun primarily for aids to beauty, our ancestors worshiped it for far more serious reasons. The sun was a god to many people — a god who rose from the netherworld in the morning and sank again in the evening. Varieties of myths and religions ascribe special powers to the sun.

In the childhood of humankind, the sun was thought to die daily in the western depths. But even more fearful to the ancients was the impending annual death of the sun and its waning light in autumn and winter. Thus, many religious festivals were associated with prayers and sacrifices to induce the sun to come back to life to give life and light to the earth.

Indeed, Christmas itself is set on December 25, the day of the ancient Roman feast of Saturnalia, which celebrated the vernal equinox in which the sun began its return journey closer to the earth to bring the light and heat essential for the new life of spring.

Christian worship has been influenced by the sun. Lighting candles on a Christmas tree is a remnant of an ancient rite to guide the sun god back to life, and the eating of Christmas plum pudding relates to a time when corn and fruit were laid on altars dedicated to the Lord of Light. St. Peter's Cathedral in Rome is placed directly East and West so that on the vernal equinox at sunrise the great doors can be thrown open to let the morning light penetrate the nave and illuminate the High Altar. And many Christians through the centuries have been buried on their backs, facing east, because in the Second Coming, Christ, the Sun of Righteousness, will come from the East to call his own in the Great Resurrection.

If we humans have been sun worshipers of one kind or another across the centuries, it is for good reason. We rightly associate the sun with light and light with life. In profound ways we have sensed, and then scientifically demonstrated, that we are dependent upon light for life and enlightenment. But reverence for the sun is not quite enough, for the sun itself is, in the biblical view, a lightholder, not the source of light itself.

I.

Let's consider *first light and life.*

In a former church, one of our leading members was lamenting his growing forgetfulness as he advanced in years. He often would joke, saying, "Don't ask me to remember what happened in the church five years ago. I hardly can even remember what I had for breakfast!"

Can you remember what you had for breakfast? Was it cereal and juice or bacon and eggs and toast? Did you have coffee and a bagel or muffin? Or did you enjoy some waffles or pancakes or French toast and fruit?

Let me suggest that ultimately what you had for breakfast was light. Yes, whatever it was you and I were eating or drinking, it was essentially light. We quite literally eat and drink light.

John Stewart Collis, in his excellent book *The Vision of Glory*, says, "The whole vegetable world may be considered as a vast mill receiving its motor power from the sun" (p. 18). Every living thing really owes existence to the living cell which runs by the process of photosynthesis. And the power, the unlimited energy source which operates photosynthesis, is light. Without it, the process of growth would cease at every level.

The average large elm tree has about six million leaves, each of them containing thousands of living cells, with all of them running on solar power. The orange tree with its fragrant blossoms, green leaves, and popular fruit, is the direct product of light. Your orange juice this morning was, quite literally, liquid light.

The amber fields of waving grain of America's heartland, pulled up from seedlings in the moist earth and ripened golden brown with summer sun, eventually end up in our morning cereal and toast, muffin or bagel. When we think of it, we were eating light, just as surely as we were drinking light from the milk from the cows who ate the grass lured into life by light, or the coffee from the beans nurtured on the Colombian bushes by the omnipresent sun. We are creatures of light.

Annie Dillard has observed that there is a "muscular energy in sunlight corresponding to the spiritual energy of wind." Says Dillard, "On a sunny day, sun's energy on a square acre of land or pond can equal 4,500 horsepower" (*Pilgrim at Tinker Creek*, pp. 120-121). So we rightly speak about solar power and in fact most of us, indeed all of us, move by solar power. The gas and oil in our cars, the tires and plastics, all ultimately derived from fossil fuel, from oil or coal, which aeons ago were living plants or organisms, fueled in photosynthesis by the sun.

And if we walk or run we do so by solar power — solar power which by photosynthesis grew the foods we ate. And we breathe the light, because the plants, by photosynthesis, take in the carbon dioxide and produce oxygen for our metabolism.

But having said all this, we are not hereby calling all people to a revival of serious sun worship. We rather are calling all people to a humble awareness of our total dependence upon light. And that light comes not ultimately from the sun, but from God, maker of heaven and earth. For the Bible does not say that the sun is the light. Instead, it says that the sun is a light holder, and that "God is light and in him is no darkness at all" (John 1:5).

Solar idolatry is alien to the biblical religions. Moses warns his people, "take care lest when you lift your eyes to Heaven and see the sun, the moon, and all the stars, you be seduced." We all might be seduced to "sun worship" for the summer tan. But in our summer and winter awareness of solar power, let us be renewed in our worship of God who is light, and the giver of all life.

II.

This brings us next to consider *light and enlightenment.*

The word "enlightenment" has had a good history in our past. We westerners have grown accustomed to our history which spoke of the "Dark Ages," when learning and advancement seemed to be at a standstill. The Italian Renaissance of the fourteenth century, the rebirth of the classics and of art, the Protestant Reformation of the sixteenth century, led eventually to the Enlightenment of the seventeenth and eighteenth centuries — a time when new discoveries and new knowledge shed more and more light into the sometimes darkened minds of people. The Enlightenment, then and now, sought to overcome the twin evils of ignorance and arrogance.

Scientists are not quite sure what light is. Is it a wave or a particle or both? We have learned that light travels at a constant 186,000 miles per second, so that each minute it travels 11,160,000 miles. Thus, it takes light from the sun about eight minutes to travel the 93,000,000 miles from there to here.

The light reaching us now from the Milky Way started thousands of years ago. And astronomers peering through the Hubbell space telescope discovered galaxies new to us whose light, just reaching us now, started perhaps millions of years ago. Consequently, most of what we see in a nighttime sky is ancient history.

The Greeks used to think that light went from the eyes to the object, but an eccentric Arab mathematician, Alhazan, living around 1000 A.D., believed light was reflected from the object. He was right, of course, and we have learned even more that not only does light need an object, all color is in the light, not in the object. The yellow of the daffodil and the red of the rose is really the capacity of those flowers to reflect that part of the spectrum of light.

However, in the biblical religions, the ultimate object for the light of God is not daffodils or roses or trees, but the human being — the man and woman fashioned in God's own image. And if the human being is dependent upon the light of God for physical life, he or she is even more dependent upon the light of God for spiritual and intellectual life.

It is regrettable that Christianity has sometimes been associated with ignorance and superstition. Skeptical historians like to point out the witch trials and wars and persecutions perpetrated in the name of Christianity. They are there, of course, to our shame and regret. But probably even more dastardly crimes have been committed over gold or oil or land or lust or craving for power.

Yet, at the heart of the Christian faith is not ignorance nor arrogance. Instead, at the heart of the Faith is the Logos of God, the very Mind of God, the Light and Life of God. Just as the sun bears light to nurture our bodies, so the Son of God who is the light of the world bears light to nurture our minds and souls.

The beautiful thing about sunlight is that we do not have to produce it. It is a gift, a gift of God's providential grace. Likewise with soul light. We do not have to produce it. It is a gift of God's providential grace. We did not have to climb up to heaven to drag the Son down, as it were. Instead, the Son came to us, in recognizable human form, to reveal the essential truths of God, and to give us eternal light and life.

Therefore, we should not despair. The darkness of ignorance and the bloodthirstiness of arrogance will not ultimately prevail. We should not let dogmatism stifle us nor pessimism suffocate us. There is always light at the end of the tunnel. We should always have hope. "The light shines in the darkness, and the darkness has not overcome it" (John 1:5).

Just think for a moment of these contrasting concepts representing light and darkness: good and evil, knowledge and ignorance, humility and arrogance, wisdom and foolishness, clarity and confusion, straight talk and double-speak, honesty and dishonesty, integrity and disintegration, truth and falsehood, clarification and obfuscation, information and misinformation. Jesus the Christ, the

Logos and Wisdom of God, has been given to us to enlighten us, to give us eternal life and salvation.

God not only creates the world in light and with light, he re-creates it in mind and spirit with the grace and truth of his own son in human form. Physically speaking, we are creatures of light. We eat it, drink it, breathe it. And about this we have no choice.

But spiritually and intellectually we do have a choice. For it is possible for our minds to be darkened by arrogance and our souls to be misled by evil. We can close ourselves off in ignorance, indifference, and small-mindedness. But if we believe, if we have faith, if we humbly seek spiritual and intellectual light and enlightenment, God is pleased to grant it.

For as John's Gospel says, "To all who received him, who believed in his name, he gave power to become children of God; who were born not of blood nor of the will of the flesh nor of the will of man, but of God" (1:12-13).

Prayer

Almighty God, source of all the universe, whose energy empowers every sun and star and galaxy, and whose logos or word holds all things together in pattern and purpose, we worship and adore you as our Maker, and look to you as the origin of all light and life. Praise be to you.

We give thanks for the splendor of summer — for birdsongs announcing the dawn, for roses red and pink and white adorning our fence rows and gardens, for impatiens proliferating into shrubs of glistening color, for oak trees and maples, stately and majestic against the sky, for tomatoes newly ripened and lettuce and onions, tomatoes and strawberries lush with color and flavor. With all the world so alive to dazzle the eye and to satisfy the palate, we can only praise you, Almighty God, giver of all good things.

However, in the grayness of winter, we confess our difficulty in keeping open to you and the world. We get set in our ways, fixed in our opinions, smug in our convictions, and narrow in our focus. We get lazy in our thinking and neglectful in our study of your Word. You always have more light and truth to reveal from your

Word, but we get distracted and become preoccupied with immediate concerns to the neglect of the eternal. Forgive our sloth and distraction and help us to see again the invigorating and encouraging truth you are waiting to give us.

And now, O God, in your mercy, be pleased to answer the inmost longings of our minds and hearts. Some of us are very discouraged and disheartened and need to see and embrace the rising sun of a new horizon. Some of us have become rigid and inflexible and need the warmth of your truth to make us pliable to receive new realities. Some of us have been enticed by lesser lights — the lure of gold, the glory of the world, and even by Satan himself who disguises himself as an angel of light. Save us, O God, from these false allurements, and keep us ever in your radiant presence that we might be always vital and enlightened. Through Jesus Christ our Lord. Amen.

4. Bread For The Journey

And the Lord said to Moses, "I have heard the murmurings of the people of Israel; say to them, 'At twilight you shall eat flesh, and in the morning you shall be filled with bread; then you shall know that I am the Lord your God.' "

— Exodus 16:11-12

It was a wonderful sight, right out of ancient history. I'll never forget it. We had just visited the hilltop ruins in ancient Pergamum in Turkey. Pergamum, famous for its 200,000-volume library 100 years before Christ, and famous for its invention of parchment, was also infamous for its worship of Caesar and its persecution of Christians who would not worship Caesar as a god.

Pergamum, center of Caesar worship, boasting a huge theater, an altar to Zeus, and a temple complex devoted to the god of healing, Asklepios, was the location of one of the famous seven churches of the book of Revelation. John writes to them to resist worshiping Caesar, a temporal king, so as to remain faithful to Christ, their eternal king. And then he promises the threatened Christians with Christ's own words: "To him who conquers I will give some of the hidden manna," the "bread from heaven" (Revelation 2:17).

So it was quite a sight and coincidence, coming down from Pergamum, to have our guide stop our bus in Bergama, the contemporary Turkish city, right in front of an old bakery. From our window I could see inside an ancient stone and brick oven with the fire blazing underneath. Our guide, a charming Turkish woman, went in and bought some bread for us, steaming hot, fresh from the oven. It was bread for the journey, like manna from heaven.

Of course the ancient Israelites escaping from Egypt were on a much more significant journey or pilgrimage than were we. And now, in the desert wilderness away from the ready food supplies of Egypt, they long for the security of three square meals a day.

Encountering the hardships and uncertainty of the desert, they idealize their past slavery and long for the fleshpots of Egypt. They complain to Moses and Aaron that they are not being given enough bread for the journey to the promised land.

In response, God provides manna for them to eat. Manna is the honey-like substance secreted by an insect after it feeds on the juice of the desert tamarisk shrub. During the night it falls to the ground, hardens, and must be gathered before the desert sun melts it. Certain Arab tribes still enjoy manna and call it the "bread of heaven."

Referring to this experience, the writer of Deuteronomy says that God was testing his people in the wilderness, to see what was in their hearts. As he put it: "And (God) humbled you and fed you with manna; ... that he might make you know that man does not live by bread alone, but that man lives by everything that proceeds from the mouth of the Lord" (Deuteronomy 8:3).

It is highly significant that Jesus himself, undergoing his temptation experiences at the beginning of his spiritual journey, quoted this very scripture. Tempted to make stones to bread, he said we do not live by bread alone, but by everything which proceeds from the mouth of the Lord. But he also taught his disciples to pray, "Give us this day our *daily* bread...."

Bread for the journey? We need daily physical bread and eternal spiritual bread.

I.

Consider first the *daily, physical bread*.

At the beginning of his ministry, it must have been greatly tempting to Jesus to succumb to the devil's suggestion that he make stones into bread. Of course, the story seems to suggest that Jesus might miraculously turn the stones into bread to feed not only his own famished body, but also the famished bodies of many of his countrymen. Later in his ministry Jesus did feed miraculously the 5,000 and 4,000 with the loaves and fishes.

Miraculous or not, Jesus could well have devoted his life to economic and agricultural reform so as to feed adequately the hungry people of the world. He literally could have changed stones into bread by helping farmers devise ways to break up the rocky ground into productive soil. When you think of it, bread does come from stones — stones pulverized into soil to grow the cereal grains. And when you think of it, that whole process is miracle enough — the growing of our daily bread.

Daily, physical bread for the daily, physical journey? Yes indeed. Jesus prayed for it and we desperately need it, especially when there are so many hungry people in the world. For example, at a recent United Nations World Summit for Children, it was noted that 150 million children under the age of five suffer from malnutrition, thirty million are living in the streets, and seven million have been driven from their homes by war and famine (*Time* Magazine, October 8, 1990, p. 41).

Daily bread for the desperately hungry of the world? You bet, we need it badly, and Christians will want to rise to the challenge to provide it. But noble as food baskets and soup kitchens may be for short term, emergency relief, the long-term solution for daily bread shall have to be more creative and all-encompassing and productive. And, thank God, just such a thing is happening in the world right now.

One of the finest examples of creative, intelligent love of neighbor in providing daily bread is Dr. Norman Borlaug, a Nobel prize-winning scientist and agronomist. A native of Iowa, Borlaug won a wrestling scholarship to the University of Minnesota where he earned a degree in forestry.

Soon Borlaug was wrestling with problems of world hunger. Emergency feeding programs wouldn't do it. So he set out to develop new kinds of grain which would be productive in Asian countries suffering from chronic food shortages. Almost single-handedly he developed the Green Revolution in Pakistan and India. He was able to increase their grain output by five times in twenty years.

His biggest miracle occurred in China. Mao invited Borlaug to China to help introduce new grains and new ways of farming. Though suffering great set-backs by Mao's Great Leap Forward (1958-60) and the Cultural Revolution (1966-76), China now leads the world in wheat, rice, and total grain production. And in many areas, China gets higher yields per acre than do Americans (*World Monitor*, October 1990, p. 44ff).

All the emergency food collections and food lifts in the world cannot compare with the revolution in food production made possible by the genius and persistence of one man — Norman Borlaug. Thank God for the daily bread he and others help provide.

II.

If we need bread for the physical journey, perhaps we need even more *spiritual bread for the spiritual journey.*

In our tour of Greece and Turkey, the stop at Pergamum was of great interest to me. I can still smell and taste that hot, fresh bread from the ancient oven.

But the next day, we were vividly reminded of the hunger for spiritual bread as we sailed into Istanbul. Several of us were up on deck early that morning, to watch as we steamed toward the famous straits of Bosporus, separating Europe and Asia.

Gradually, the famous city came into view in the beautiful sunrise — the famous city, Istanbul, or Constantinople as Emperor Constantine named it in 326 A.D., or Byzantium as it was called before that. Constantine had decided to move the capital from Rome to this strategic site, more central to the Empire. It soon became a magnificent city, with art and architectural treasures from everywhere.

A little earlier, in 313 A.D., Constantine had issued his famous Edict of Toleration, allowing Christianity to be "tolerated" as a legal religion for the first time in its history. And then in the neighboring town of Nicea, Constantine called the famous Council of Nicea in 325 A.D., from which we have the standard Nicene Creed. Soon after that, the Emperor authorized the construction of a Christian church, the Hagia Sophia, the Church of the Holy Wisdom.

On deck early that August morning, we gradually saw it come into view — the Hagia Sophia, high on the hill overlooking the Bosporus, glowing in its pink, dusty-rose exterior in the rising sun. The Hagia Sophia — how I had longed for years to see it, this famous, huge Church of Christendom, where emperors had been crowned and millions had worshiped over the centuries. No, it was not the structure Constantine had built. That was destroyed. But this Hagia Sophia, now a Turkish museum, dated from 537 A.D.

Think of it, over 1,400 years old, standing as a magnificent witness of our need for spiritual bread.

As if that famous site were not enough, close by was the towering magnificence of the famous Blue Mosque, named for the beautiful blue tiles on the interior walls. Here for centuries, thousands upon thousands of Muslims have gathered to pray and to hear the word of Allah preached to them. Another magnificent testimony to our need for spiritual bread for our spiritual pilgrimage.

Despite those magnificent structures in Istanbul and, despite the completion of the majestic National Cathedral in Washington, D.C., there is growing evidence of spiritual famine in the world and especially in our country. We are spiritually gaunt, ethically malnourished and starving for real, life-sustaining values and principles.

Consider, for example, the plight of American children. Here is a day's worth of destiny for them. "Every eight seconds of the school day, a child drops out. Every 26 seconds a child runs away from home. Every 47 seconds, a child is abused or neglected. Every 67 seconds, a teenager has a baby. Every seven minutes, a child is arrested for a drug offense. Every 36 minutes, a child is killed or injured by a gun. Every day 135,000 children bring guns to school" (*Time, op cit.*, p. 42).

Our education system is in real trouble. Former Education Secretary, Lauro Cavazos, calls our student performance "dreadfully inadequate." And from both the inner-city and affluent suburbs comes, says one writer, "a drumbeat of stories about tin-pot principals who cannot be fired, beleaguered teachers with unmanageable work-loads and illiterate graduates with abysmal test scores" (*ibid.*, p. 44).

And lest we delude ourselves, the problems extend to the affluent families of city and suburb. If we are not present with our children we try to substitute with money. "We supply kids with things in the absence of family," says a school administrator. "We used to build dreams for them, but now we buy Nintendo toys, and Reebok sneakers" (*ibid.*, p. 45). And in affluent areas we have drug and alcohol use, eating disorders, suicide attempts, and general despair and apathy.

If adults lament the absence of values, we are to be reminded that our children reflect what they learn from us and our principles and priorities. As one writer put it: "A society whose values are entirely material is not likely to breed a generation of poets; anti-intellectualism and indifference to education do not inspire rocket scientists." And the writer asks, "Where is the leader who will seize the opportunity to do what is both smart and worthy, and begin returning policy to focus on children and intercept trouble before it breeds?" (*ibid.*, p. 40).

Who indeed? Well for one, the Church ought to step up again to its leadership roles in education, ethics, morals, families, and lasting values. The Church, often so anemic and drowsy, needs to revisit the Hagia Sophia, the "holy wisdom," to wake up to its historic leadership task.

So we must ask, are your children in church and church school, in youth and education programs? Are they really learning spiritual truths and ethical values? From whom? You?

And have you read the Bible lately or read a responsible book on ethics or morals or wrestled lately with some of the great ideas of history? Or are you wasting away from spiritual malnutrition?

Daily bread and physical bread? How desperately we need it. We pray for the Norman Borlaugs of the world and rouse ourselves from simplistic, romantic, Band-Aid solutions to world agricultural and economic reform.

Spiritual bread, eternal bread, giving nourishment to mind and soul? How desperately we need it. Let us pray for our schools and churches and families that they might wake up before it is too late and our civilization dies from spiritual emptiness.

Prayer

Eternal God, who has made the world in grandeur and majesty, and who has set in motion the mysterious processes of life, seed bearing seed, bringing forth after its own kind, we praise you for wonders beyond our knowing, and thank you for the gift of life beyond our fathoming.

Loving Father, who dwells beyond the limits of all space and time, who yet has willed to express yourself in the world in human image, you have made us for space and time and have placed us within the vicissitudes of history. From conception to birth, from childhood to adolescence, through adulthood to old age, we are caught up in gaining and getting, growing and developing, and then in sighing and dying.

In our pilgrimage, feed us, O Lord, our daily bread. The amber fields of waving grain, the golden corn in harvest moon, the fruit of the vine flowing robust red — all remind us of the providence and intricacy of your creative power. You make us with the complex abilities of smelling and touching, tasting and digesting, and then create the world in a riot of color and taste and smell and give us a body and mind to see and digest and appropriate it all for our growth and enjoyment. Praise be to you, O Lord, for all our daily breads which truly are manna from heaven.

If you have made us with bodies craving food for growth and development, you have made us with minds and souls craving spiritual bread for hungers and longings deeper than physical.

Look mercifully upon our frequent emptiness of soul and vacancy of mind. Anxious in our getting and spending, we too easily lay waste our powers, coming to the close of the day still spiritually famished.

But in Jesus, your word of life, the true bread for the soul, come down from heaven, you have promised to feed us, to satisfy us, and fulfill us with the life which is eternal. Help us to be open to you to receive this heavenly manna so as to be nourished for the steadfast pilgrimage of faith, hope, and love. In Christ's name we pray. Amen.

5. What Will You Have — Dancing Or Fasting?

We piped to you, and you did not dance; We wailed, and you did not mourn.   — Matthew 11:17

Across the sea, along the shore,
In numbers more and ever more,
From lonely hut and busy town,
The valley through, the mountain down,
What was it ye went out to see,
Ye silly folk of Galilee?
The reed that in the wind doth shake?
The weed that washes in the lake?
The reeds that waver, the weeds that float?
A young man preaching in a boat.

Arthur Hugh Clough has it right. It was no flimsy reed, no wavering swamp grass or cattails blowing in the wind those crowds went out to see. Those humble folk of old Judea, those seeking multitudes of ancient Galilee were not drawn into the wilderness to hear a political chameleon who changed speeches with the mood of the day.

John, thundering at the riverside, Jesus preaching from the mount, teaching from the boat, and the people heard them gladly. They preached and taught as men with authority. Unlike would-be leaders of our day, they did not take opinion polls to find out what people believed and then proclaim that's what they believed also. They did not get their convictions from the offices of Harris or Gallup or the *New York Times*. Jesus and John were authentic because their convictions arose out of a life of intense prayer, reflection, study, and experience with people and power.

What was it ye went out to see,
Ye silly folk of Galilee?

The reeds that waver, the weeds that float?
A young man preaching in a boat.

John and Jesus — authentic men, true men, who, unlike so many leaders interested in feathering their own nest, spoke their message without regard for the consequences. That's why John was in prison. Herod, although he admired John, could take no more of the truth. So he locked him up, and later, chopped off his head. Herod knew better than to attempt to bribe John or to place him in exile. No wavering reed in the wind, he knew John could be silenced only by death.

So it would be also with Jesus. Silenced only by death. And why? Because Jesus and John were calling men and women, boys and girls, into the Kingdom, not of men, but of God. Jesus' method was so different from John's, that John in his prison cell wondered if in fact he was the Messiah. Have no doubt, said Jesus to John; the blind see, the lame walk, and the poor have good news preached to them. The Kingdom is arriving for all who will receive it. And so it was by two different methods, "dancing and fasting," the Kingdom arrived.

I.

John tried fasting. His way to the Kingdom was through asceticism and prayer and the solitary life. He gave up the customary pleasures and comforts to concentrate on what he understood to be the life of the Spirit. John forsook the pleasures of marriage and family, and the ordinary pursuits of business and social life. Through rigorous discipline and social withdrawal, he attempted to avoid the pitfalls of compromise.

While John earned the admiration of many, he received the accusation of others. A man like that must be mad, they said. He's out of his mind, perhaps even possessed by a demon. He fasts so often he has lost his perspective. The solitary life isn't good for a man. His prayers have become too intense and he has grown too critical of the world.

And so it went. The various social groups accused him of being a little odd and much too fanatical about the Kingdom of God.

Nevertheless, some were enticed to withdraw from the dinner party, cocktail lounge circuit. John's wilderness life had a certain allurement — away from the crowds, close to nature, sensitive to the winds of the hills, the fragrances of the flowers. Who of us has not thought of sailing off with Robert Louis Stevenson to a South Pacific island or stealing away like Anne Morrow Lindbergh to discover the "gift from the sea." Maybe in solitude and fasting and prayer we could find the Kingdom. Perhaps our vision of God could be clarified, our understanding of Christ enhanced.

Is fasting the way for you? Have you ever come back from the indulgence of the Mardi Gras prepared to give up something for Lent? I heard about some high school girls who were giving up candy. One man said he was giving up alcohol for Lent. Oh, I chided him, you plan on sobering up for these forty days? No, he said, I need to lose some weight!

Fasting is a good way to focus on the Kingdom. Those who have tried it have found that it heightens awareness and increases sensitivity. Concentration often is enhanced. Insight is deepened. Self-deception burns away and the stark truths about the world become more plainly visible. It can be a frightening, life-shaking experience of reorientation.

Many people in John's day found it to be too much. With the intensity of fasting and prayer they became both aware and afraid of the forces within themselves. Others were too threatened by the thought of being alone with themselves, afraid of being alone with God, fearful of pulling aside the social fabrications to look at the truth of their souls. And so the stereo always is on, or the television, or the transistor radio, or the computer.

A religion of such personal intensity was more than they could bear. It was too shattering to see the untruthfulness of people, too devastating to see how little people really cared for one another, and how little difference it made whether they lived or died. Like a jet plane approaching the intensity of the sound barrier, they pulled back from the turbulence they were seeing, without pressing on through to the peace and calm and heavenly perspective on the other side of the barrier. For on the other side of the barrier we receive strength to see how selfish and unloving and uncaring we have been. We understand how unworthy of trust we have been, how deceptive and self-deceiving, how ready to manipulate and use others to our advantage and their disadvantage.

I saw a cartoon of a man returning home from work, greeting his wife, saying, "I feel as though I really got ahead today. I was exploited by four people, but I exploited nine."

Beyond the sound barrier we can see and reaffirm the world, but this time with a heart that has been shaken clean in the turbulence of self-examination, and with a mind that has been clarified with the intensity of honest introspection. We have entered the Kingdom of truth and light. Will you come to the Kingdom by way of fasting?

II.

Dancing advocates found a good leader in Jesus. Unlike John, Jesus was no social recluse. The contrary. Jesus enjoyed good times and often attended wedding feasts and dinner parties. He apparently loved the communal life as he and his disciples traveled and lived together, frequently being accompanied by assorted hangers-on. So much did he enjoy and participate in social occasions that his opponents tried to label him as a glutton and drunkard. The label was untrue, of course, but he was seen often enough at parties to make people wonder.

If John was austere and solitary, Jesus was amiable and sociable. If John called people into the Kingdom by way of asceticism and severe discipline, Jesus beckoned by way of the feast and the gladness of the dinner party. If, as a loner, John's vision of the Kingdom was enhanced, Jesus, as a social person, knew the insight and sense of identity which came from a community and the give and take of stories and conversation.

What do you plan to give up for Lent? Some would say, I'm giving up being alone. I'm putting aside thinking of myself all the time. Instead of complaining about my aches and pains, I'm going to listen to someone else tell about his or hers, and help them gain a sense of release. What do you plan to give up for Lent? Others would say, I'm going to come out of the desert places of selfishness to share with someone else — to give some food or money or kindly words of encouragement. I'm going to put aside for the moment preoccupation with my career to help someone else with his or hers. The Kingdom of God is not just solitariness, but a community of trust and mutual burden bearing.

But if John was criticized for being too monkish, Jesus was criticized for being too sociable. If John was disliked because he always turned down party invitations, Jesus was scorned because he rarely missed a party. The critics refused to see the Kingdom through John's eyes, but they also refused to see in it the methodology of Jesus.

For many people, a religious man having a good time was a contradiction. A somber countenance gave a much more pious impression. Wise religious leaders have learned not to laugh too heartily or to enjoy life too much. It gives the impression they are not enough concerned with the Kingdom.

Ironically, the hedonists, the pleasure-seekers, really want a religious leader who is not too happy or congenial. They may say they like a good-time Charlie and a leader who is like one of the boys, but in their heart of hearts they really do not. They much prefer a somewhat somber leader to serve as a model for their alter ego and guilty conscience.

Hedonists could not conceive a religious leader having a good time like themselves, for they knew that in their pleasure, they were not religious. In their good times they were seeking not the Kingdom of God, but the Kingdom of pleasure, that blissful realm where all the impulses and instincts had full expression.

The difference between themselves and Jesus was what their good times meant. For Jesus, feasts and parties were symbols and signs of the coming Kingdom of God of which he was an agent. For the hedonists, the good times were an effort to cover up the dread, the feeling that life and the Kingdom had passed them by. They had come to a deep, silent despair about life, and were overlaying the despair with parties and dancing. Thus, in all their search for the true community, the Kingdom of God, they never really found it because they never opened up to true sharing and listening and loving and caring. For all their sociability, they were more lonely than John. What will you have — dancing or fasting?

Some say you can attract more flies with honey than with vinegar. They are right. John believed you also attracted more corruption, shame, and hypocrisy with honey. He knew words of vinegar were needed to cut the overlaid deceit and self-deception. John was not interested in attracting flies. He was interested in leading people to the cleansing and liberating experience of repentance.

Nonetheless, people thought he was out of his mind, taking his religion far too seriously. They proposed he relax, settle down, enjoy some of the finer things of life. Life and society are not as bad as they seem, John. Enjoy, indulge yourself a bit. You have been too long in the wilderness fasting and praying. You have lost balanced perspective, they said.

Jesus, on the other hand, came not so much with vinegar, but with honey. And he attracted all sorts of flies, even prostitutes, publicans, and sinners. The vinegar of judgment and retribution had been replaced with the sweetness of love and forgiveness. The common people heard him gladly and flocked to his side — until they learned how encompassing true love really is; until they discovered the cost of forgiveness. Then, as with John, many backed away.

They had expected religion to be an accoutrement, a nice 14-carat gold plating on the fundamental structure of their lives. They assumed Jesus was endorsing all their manners and ethics when he entered into wedding feasts and dinner parties with great zest and enjoyment. They presumed he, like they, had compromised his ideals and had built up a solid core of calculating cynicism with which to approach life. And when Jesus' real commitment became known, they tried to assassinate his character by dismissing him as a glutton and winebibber.

God once again is calling us to his Kingdom. For some he calls through mourning and fasting and solitude. Others he calls through fun and feasts and community. But if we do not want to listen to the truth, we will, like spoiled children, find all sorts of ways to avoid John and Jesus. We will criticize the method to avoid the meaning. We will berate the messenger to avoid the message.

Or with gladness and singleness of heart, we will be open and receptive to the peace and beauty and power of his word for our lives. By any means, dancing or fasting, God wills to come to us. But it is up to us to receive him into our lives.

> *What was it ye went out to see,*
> *Ye silly folk of Galilee?*
>
> *The reeds that waver, the weeds that float?*
> *A young man preaching in a boat.*

Prayer

In the first, fine, careless capture of the morning of the first day of the rest of our lives, we perceive your presence and power, Lord God. You've got the whole world in your hands, butterflies and babies, girls and daffodils, unfolding with beauty and grace in this delicate space, earth, our revolving home.

In our hands, we've got our old days, agonies and memories, guilt and regret, despair and distress. The life begun in beauty has its marks of ugliness, the days of blissful innocence have succumbed into long years of experience doing what we know we shouldn't, not doing what we know we should.

We've come to you, Spirit of us all — with our weariness and reluctance to get out of bed, our hassle at home, and lack of time for the second cup — with all that we've come, O Present One, partly out of duty, but more deeply, because we know our real need of your sustenance. Life, with all its tragedies and perplexities, baffles us beyond our ability to cope, and we become aware of demonic powers so vast, so encompassing, we sense ourselves caught up and entangled in their grip.

We come, O loving Father, for the liberation and freedom which you give in your love and grace. Break these shackles which too long have bound us — these inward fears which grip our very souls, these desperate feelings of emptiness, our distressing sense of powerlessness. Accustomed to commanding our ship, we feel now we are being carried along in massive tides which laugh at our powers and scorn our futile efforts at self-control.

O God, who reverses the flow of evil, and who overcomes the tides of bondage and sorrow which engulf the human soul, bring now the dawn of a new day of liberation, a true one, the overcoming of the foes which beset us. Let this be a new day for us. Let this be the first day of the rest of our lives. Breathe into us your peace and presence which enables us to cope and to rise above our crippling ways of thinking, degrading ways of behaving, our negative approach to problem solving, our lack of faith in the power of your good to overcome the evil in our lives. O God, let this be the day when we enter your Kingdom anew. Through Jesus Christ our Lord. Amen.

6. Faith And Fast-Food Religion

Jesus said to the twelve, "Do you also wish to go away?" Simon Peter answered him, "Lord to whom shall we go? You have the words of eternal life."
— John 6:67-68

It was many years ago when he told me. It was somewhat unbelievable then, but surely not now. My wife's uncle was a buyer for a large restaurant chain. "Our research shows us," he told me, "that in a few years American businessmen and many businesswomen will be eating out twice a day. More than that," he said, "there will be a proliferation of fast-food chains, like you won't believe."

Well, I believe it. His prophecy proved to be more true than perhaps even their researchers dreamed. People do eat out a great deal. Most every American child knows the delights of a Big Mac or a Whopper and fries. Domino's Pizza will deliver in thirty minutes or it's free, and Kentucky Fried Chicken can be eaten in or taken home for the whole family. Chicken McNuggets and Dunkin' Donuts and bagels by the billions are a part of the fast-food phenomenon. America is eating on the run.

And in some respects Americans are taking their religion on the run. Some years ago, Episcopal priest Malcolm Boyd published a book of prayers titled *Are You Running With Me, Jesus?* In my mind the title always provoked the image of a marathon runner with Jesus running up alongside to give him a quick drink or morale-boosting prayer, then fading to the side while the runner rushed on toward his goal. Boyd seemed to imply Jesus' main role in life was to rush up to help us with whatever need we might have, and then fade into the background while we pursued our goals.

That's the way it has become with much of American religion, says Dr. Leander Keck of Yale University in his book *The Church Confident*. Instead of praising God we expect God to praise us. We expect God to help us reach our predetermined goals of success and high self-esteem. Like important busy executives, we come to worship to give God an audience, telling him in effect, okay, you've got sixty minutes to make your sale.

Better yet, many of us prefer a drive-thru, take-out, pick-up religion of convenience for people on the go. It should be pre-cooked, pre-packaged, ready to pop in the microwave to eat instantly along with instant soup and instant coffee. That's about it, God, we say. We're a consumer-oriented culture on the fast track to success and glory. So when we come to your take-out window, you better have it ready to go. And at best, you've got sixty minutes to make your case.

I.

It may surprise you to know that *fast-food religion appears in the Bible.*

Recall the famous story of the exodus of the Hebrews from Egypt in 1290 B.C. Soon after their miraculous escape with Moses through the Red Sea, and then the beginning of their arduous trek through the Sinai desert, the Hebrews began to murmur and complain.

As their rations of food began to run out, they started looking longingly back toward the land of their slavery and bondage. With hunger pangs growing ever more intense, they yearned for the leeks and onions and fleshpots of Egypt. At least in Egypt, they complained to Moses, we knew where our next meal was coming from.

And then the fast-food miracle occurred. God provided fresh each morning manna from heaven, a honey cake, bread-like substance adhering to the desert tamarisk bush. There it was each morning. No cooking necessary. Just go over to the take-out bush and eat!

But the Israelites got tired even of this bread from heaven. They longed for some real meat. After all, they complained, you can be vegetarian only so long. So God caused quail to land near them on their migrating routes. And since the quail were exhausted, they were easy to catch and cook. No, it wasn't exactly instant pheasant under glass, but it was a kind of take-out and heat-up perpetual dinner.

But fast-food didn't quite do it for them. They still were murmuring and complaining. But Moses warned them in a sermon, saying, "God humbled you and let you hunger and fed you with manna, which you did not know, nor did your fathers know; that he might make you know that man does not live by bread alone, but that man lives by everything that proceeds out of the mouth of the Lord" (Deuteronomy 8:3). But they still didn't quite get it.

The same is true in the time of Jesus. In the classic temptations text, Jesus, after his fasting in the desert wilderness, is tempted to turn stones into bread. The temptation is powerfully symbolic in many ways. It is not just a matter of Jesus satisfying his own hunger, but of using his Messianic powers to institute massive economic reform to feed the hungry multitudes of the world. In other words, the best thing he could do for the world would be to provide bread, physical bread, bread of this world for the good life in this world.

One can understand the temptation. One vision of the Messianic Age from the prophet, Amos, predicts the day: "When the one who plows shall overtake the one who reaps, and the treader of grapes the one who sows the seed" (9:13). Materialistic abundance, the rich benefits of the good life, a full stomach and bank account are what it's all about, they argued. Turn those stones to bread, Jesus, and do it fast, because we want it all, and we want it all now. Are you running with me, Jesus?

Another biblical fast-food episode forms the background of our text from John's Gospel. Jesus had just miraculously fed 5,000 men plus women and children. The next morning, the crowd came rushing around the northern end of the Sea of Galilee looking for Jesus. Why, you might ask. Well, because they had had a fast-food, miraculous dinner the night before. Now they were looking for a free, fast-food miraculous breakfast — their version of Egg McMuffin and coffee.

Knowing what they were after, it was then he advised them in the words of Isaiah, "Do not labor for the food which perishes, but for the food which endures to eternal life, which the Son of Man will give to you...." (John 6:27; Isaiah 55:2). Faith is more than fast-food religion and instant, effort-free gratification. As Jesus, echoing Moses, said to the Tempter, "Man does not live by bread alone, but by every word which proceeds out of the mouth of God," so he would tell us (Matthew 4:4). Rather, we should seek for the bread of eternal life which he wishes to give us.

II.

If the Bible speaks of fast-food religion, it wishes even more to draw our attention to the religion of feasts and banquets and dinner parties. *The religion of faith is really gourmet religion.*

Some of you will recall the absolutely delightful movie, *Babette's Feast*. A masterpiece of art and symbolism, the film depicts a puritanical Protestant sect of Jutland, the northwestern peninsula of Denmark. Accustomed to a dark, cold, damp, and gray existence, their theology and their food reflected their environment.

Then Babette, an exiled French chef, appeared in their midst and determined to prepare for them an absolutely exquisite gourmet feast. Weeks in preparation, she ordered wines from France, spices from Europe, and exquisite foods from everywhere, paying for it out of the lottery prize she had won. In due time, those gourmet-deprived, gray, pleasure-denying Protestant Jutlanders were in the seventh heaven of gastronomical delights. And the feast became a symbol of Jesus' Last Supper, offering himself, as Babette offered herself, her talents and skills and money for the physical and spiritual nurturance of those deprived people.

So too Jesus would have us come to the rich, gourmet banquet of faith. But as with Babette, it takes patience and preparation and a willingness to wait upon the Lord. University of Chicago's Allan Bloom thinks it's precisely those qualities we have lost in America. We have lost the centrality of the Bible and faith and a gripping inner life, says Bloom and "the dreariness of the family's spiritual landscape passes belief." He says, "People sup together, (usually on the run, we might add), travel together, but they do not think together (and we might add, pray together)" (*The Closing of the American Mind*, pp. 57, 58). Our spiritual life too often resembles the gray dreariness of those Jutlanders in *Babette's Feast*.

Faith, real faith, takes some time, some reflection, some introspection and confession and contrition. It takes some serious Bible study, some discussion and sharing, some confrontation with new ideas, and sometimes, it takes a crisis or two to make us think there may be more to life than success and a specialized competence.

But the 5,000 Jesus fed a fast-food dinner, now looking for a fast-food breakfast, were disappointed. They were hoping for a new Moses who would give them fast-food manna and quail every day. But Jesus told them he was the bread of heaven, his message was the true bread of life. You need to eat of this bread to really live. And many, seeing he was not going to perform another miracle of fast-food, turned away. They wanted a quick-fix, drive-thru, take-out faith. Jesus was calling them to a feast — himself.

Jesus was the man of destiny with economic and political power his for the taking, to actualize the good life here and now. But he gave up his life, his Messianic complex, his ego, his fascination with money and power, to worship the only true source of life and power — God himself.

And as a result, God has made him the very spiritual bread of life for us all. So Jesus has stimulated more books and art, music and literature, architecture and medicine than any figure in history. What he has done is provide a veritable feast for mind and soul, gourmet food for the spiritual life. Jesus saw early on what it takes many a lifetime to see: "Man does not live by bread alone, but by every word which proceeds from the mouth of God."

Fast-food religion? It may be just the thing for some. But for faith, God has planned gourmet food. He invites us to his everlasting table in the Psalmist's ancient words:

> *O taste and see how gracious*
> *the Lord is,*
> *blessed is the man that*
> *trusteth in him.* — Psalm 34:8 (KJV)

True faith and religion is not the McDonald's drive-thru after all. It's Babette's feast!

Prayer

Eternal God, mind of the universe and our mentor, from whom comes every good and perfect thought, and in whose presence darkness and confusion dissipate, we give you thanks and praise that you have not left us desolate nor abandoned us to chaos. Everywhere we look we behold your beneficent intelligence at work in all living things — from bacteria to buffalo, from ants to antelope. In wisdom you made them all, and in patient mercy you sustain them.

And you have made us — we know not how — a little lower than the angels, to have dominion over the earth and to govern ourselves and the world with wisdom. But in your holy presence we must confess our readiness to follow instinct and passion, our tendency to allow fleeting feelings to hold sway over considered judgment. Forgive our impulsive ways, our compulsions and obsessions, and bring us to the considered truth and wisdom of our Lord Jesus Christ.

O God, who loves us each as if there were only one to love, attend to the deepest yearnings of our hearts, and heed the inmost longings of our souls. Grant us insight to know your will and wisdom to do it. Help us to know that it is in love and worship of you we find our true self and that our souls are restless until they rest confidently in you. Through Jesus Christ our Lord. Amen.

7. Parties, Perfumes, And The Poor

Jesus said, "Let her alone, let her keep it for the day of my burial. The poor you always have with you, but you do not always have me."
— John 12:7-8

It was an unusual experience. It happened some years ago in New York City on an elevator. I was working and living in East Harlem at the time. But I had gone to midtown for a meeting with an attorney friend in his high-rise office building.

So it caught me by surprise, an experience totally unexpected. I stepped on the elevator in slack time in mid-afternoon. The doors closed on me and the one other person in the elevator — an attractive woman. As we ascended, it happened. The scent of the beautiful woman's perfume wafted over to my side of the elevator.

And surprise of surprises! It made me think not of her, but of another woman I dated years ago and miles away in high school. It was the same fragrance. And as I took it in, my mind went back to a lovely and pretty young girl I had the privilege of dating as a high school boy.

In that sense, the perfume was sacramental. It had the power not only to point to a reality beyond itself; it had the power to cause me to participate in a reality beyond itself. It not only suggested the young lady I used to date, it flooded my mind with memories of happy times and laughter and the delights of young and innocent attraction. It was the power of perfume.

So too the perfume of our scripture text. As I read the text, I do not experience the fragrance they experienced at that dinner party in Bethany, just outside Jerusalem twenty centuries ago. No, I am not drawn back by the sensory apparatus to see what they saw and feel what they felt.

Yet, there is a power to that perfume, an allure in that imagined fragrance which draws us across the centuries to a formative event in the life of the faith. For as the Gospel says, the act of sharing that costly perfume that special night at that dinner party would be spoken of throughout the world. And so it is, here we are, 10,000 miles and twenty-one centuries removed from the event, and we are still talking about it.

So let's take a look at parties, perfumes, and the poor.

I.

Consider first the *parties*.

During Lent, the traditional season of fasting, we sometimes find ourselves talking about the feasts of the Kingdom and about parties. I am reminded of the lady who decided to combine the fasting of Lent with dieting and exercise to lose weight. She consulted the doctor, and he advised horseback riding. She tried it and it worked. The horse lost eighteen pounds! In a season when it is customary to give up something to show our devotion to God, our text speaks of happy times and extravagant expenditures. And yet, there it is, the story of Jesus at a dinner party, just days before his crucifixion.

The religious people of Jesus' time had lots of problems with Jesus' concept of religion. To tell you the truth, John the Baptist fit the more acceptable image of the genuine prophet and holy man, living as he did, in the wilderness away from the comforts of family and civilization.

John preached a fiery and stern message of repentance, which matched his piercing eyes and his penetrating gaze into the heart and soul of his hearers. Fasting on the austere wilderness foods of locusts and wild honey, John spoke of a religion austere, spare, and severe. "Repent, you sinners. The one coming after me will baptize not with water, but with spirit and with fire!"

No wonder then that John's followers — many of them — were disappointed with Jesus. Where was the fire? No wonder then that Jesus came under criticism by many of the religious leaders of the time. If John the Baptist was austere, Jesus seemed lenient. If John was incessantly demanding, Jesus seemed endlessly accepting. If John urged everyone to toe the line and obey the law to the fullest, Jesus seemed almost to ignore the law and to concentrate on good times.

And this showed up most in his feasts and dinner parties. That's what made many people wonder about the genuineness of his religion. He would eat with just about anybody. Think of Zacchaeus, the short but very wealthy tax collector. Remember, Zacchaeus, a Jew employed by the Romans to collect the hated taxes, would be hated by the citizens as a turncoat and traitor, as an exploiter and oppressor worse than the Romans. Since he was one of their own turned against them, he was worse than the enemy.

Yet Jesus invited himself to Zacchaeus' house to dine, and as a result changed Zacchaeus' life forever. He repaid fourfold all those he defrauded and vowed to help the poor. All because Jesus broke the rules, crossed the boundaries of exclusive dining habits, inviting himself to a dinner party with a despised outsider.

Jesus repeated the practice over and over again. One time he even dined with Simon, the leper. All lepers were religiously impure in those days, so any self-respecting religious leader would avoid them like the plague they were. But not Jesus. He not only healed the leper, he ate with him, breaking the barriers of religious and social snobbishness.

On and on the story goes. Whether it's at the wedding feast in Cana of Galilee where water was turned to wine, or entertaining in his own home in Capernaum, or at a dinner party with Mary, Martha, and Lazarus in Bethany, Jesus loved parties. So much so, his enemies called him a glutton and a drunkard. He wasn't that, of course, but compared to John the Baptist, he seemed to be.

It is this practice of eating with all people that is at the heart of Jesus' idea of the Kingdom of God, says Jesus Seminar scholar, John Dominic Crossan. God is interested in everyone, not just the select few who have the time and money to practice all the minutiae of religious fastidiousness. So in feast after feast, in healing after healing, in parable after parable, Jesus strives to break down the barriers between races, clans, religions, gender, and social classes.

As he put it, people shall come from the East and West, South and North, and sit down together in the banquet feast of the Kingdom of God. "In Christ there is neither Jew nor Greek, slave nor free, male nor female, but all are one in Christ," said Paul picking up on the universalization theme (Galatians 3:28). And nineteen centuries later John Oxenham sang of it in his hymn,

> *In Christ, there is no East or West,*
> *In him, no South or North,*
> *But one great fellowship divine,*
> *Throughout the whole wide earth.*

II.

But the beautiful thing about this particular party described in our text is the *perfume*. This dinner party was blessed with the pleasing and stimulating fragrance of an expensive perfume.

All four Gospels have an account of this dinner party, or perhaps we have varied accounts of at least two dinner parties. One Gospel speaks of a dinner with Simon the Pharisee. While Jesus is reclining at table with the men (women would not be allowed), a woman slips in and begins to wash Jesus' feet with her tears and dry them with her hair.

Simon, the religiously pure and righteous man, who would have had the admiration of John the Baptist, sniffs in snobbish comment saying, surely Jesus could not be the famous holy man they claim he is, because he is letting this harlot, this woman of the street, perform such a sensuous act. No self-respecting holy man would allow such a display.

But Jesus said to Simon, "Simon do you not see what is happening? When I came, you failed to greet me with the customary Oriental kiss, but she, since she came, has not ceased kissing me; and kissing not my cheeks, but of all things, kissing my feet. And speaking of feet, when I came you did not extend to me the customary Near Eastern courtesy of washing my feet with soothing water from your well. But this woman, at whom you sneer, has not ceased washing my feet, not with water from the well, but with tears from her eyes."

Jesus went on to speak of the power of what was happening. Her sins, which were many, were forgiven. She loves much, said Jesus, because she has been forgiven much. And the fragrance of her love extended throughout the dinner party and then all around the world to illustrate what the gospel is all about.

It is about forgiveness and acceptance, and inclusiveness and love. So many of us think of ourselves as too good for this woman. The unacceptable peoples of the world are not a part of our crowd. We prefer to socialize with the rich and famous, the successful and powerful. If we do not put religious boundaries between ourselves and others, we put socio-economic, class boundaries.

But people in Alcoholics Anonymous and Narcotics Anonymous and other Twelve Step groups know what it is to be accepted and accepting. They know what it is to be lifted up by a power greater than their own. And who of us have not, at times, felt rejected, left out, discriminated against or excluded? But the good news is that with Jesus and the Kingdom of God, it is always open house. "Come, sit down and dine and laugh and sing with me in the Kingdom of God," says Jesus.

III.

But then, of course, we have the *poor*. Yes, said Jesus, the poor you have with you always, but you will not always have me with you. And so Jesus not only justifies parties in the presence of poverty and the poor, he even justifies perfumes.

Let's return to the scene of the dinner party of our text. Reclining with Lazarus and others at table in the Bethany home of Mary, Martha, and Lazarus (Lazarus now raised from the dead), Jesus and the others are served by Martha. But Mary this time is not sitting at the feet of Jesus to learn (to the consternation of Martha adhering to the traditional female role). No, this time she is anointing Jesus' feet (not his head which would suggest his role as Messiah) with very expensive perfume — about eleven ounces of it. It would take a day laborer a year's worth of wages to pay for it. And Mary used it all — anointing Jesus' feet soon to be pierced with nails, and then wiped his feet with her hair. It was a loving act of sensuous and devoted extravagance.

The financiers were of course immediately up in arms. And guess who was the leading financier? It was Judas, the treasurer of the group. He objected immediately to this lavish display of love and devotion, complaining the perfume could have been sold and the money given to the poor. What he really meant, John's Gospel tells us, is that if the perfume had been sold, the proceeds would have gone into the campaign chest where he, as treasurer of the group, would have had control of it. More than that, he was a thief, says John, and would have used the money for himself, and not the poor.

Yet this act of lavish love and devotion is at the heart of true religion and true human relationships. Many of us will remember Tevye in *Fiddler on the Roof* when he repeatedly asks his wife if she loves him. She responds by grumbling about how she cooks his meals, washes his clothes, looks after his house, and raises the kids. But Tevye persists, "Do you love me?" His wife recites another long list of the wifely and motherly duties performed day after day, month after month, but without much of a smile or sense of grace.

But Tevye, of course, is looking for passion, for feeling, for that first fine careless rapture of letting go into the bliss of love. But what he seems to get is duty, performed in resigned drudgery and routine, executed with righteous indignation.

But not with Mary and Jesus. She unreservedly, unabashedly, and extravagantly expresses herself in the carefree abandon of love toward the one who has captivated her heart and mind. Putting aside propriety and rigidity, she allows passion to dictate performance, and heartfelt devotion to supercede ritual duty. So the lavish, expensive perfume wafted its fragrance through the house and into the streets and across the world and into our time, into this very moment.

And in this moment it would tell us that in worship and prayer, in openness to the Spirit of God, in humility, kneeling before the Almighty in need of grace — in such moments is the truth of life and love to be found. If there are some who believe music is essentially notes and strings and mathematics, those with ears to hear know that music is ecstasy and thralldom, inspiration and insight. All great music is truly soul music.

If there are some who believe art is essentially ink on paper, oil on canvas, or hammer on stone, those with eyes to see know that great art is deep, divine recognition of kindred perceptions of reality felt and experienced above the tedium of routine and the drudgery of duty.

So too, the entrancement of the religious vision. When we truly meet Jesus in the depths of our deep need, and gaze upon the immense tenderness and see the depth of understanding and forgiveness in his eyes, we are then ready to break out the best champagnes and the most expensive perfumes in heartfelt, soulfelt devotion.

You may recall reading of the very well-to-do woman of New York City when she was remodeling her very expensive Manhattan apartment. Hundreds of thousands of dollars were spent on every luxurious detail. And her bathroom was a showplace of opulence, drawing oohs and aahs from the reporters.

But there it was — something none of the sated, hardened reporters had ever seen. It was a small refrigerator in the bathroom next to the very large bathtub. It was not for cold drinks, but for cold perfume! Said the lady to the reporters, "I simply cannot imagine getting out of my hot bath without being able to splash myself with cold perfume!"

The poor of the world do indeed have a claim against the excessive opulence of that woman, but they do not have a claim against Mary, said Jesus. Let all the bottom-line, hard-nosed, dollar-sign-only financiers put away their calculators and balance sheets, because, says Jesus, true religion is not first of all money, even money for the poor. True religion is first of all true devotion — lavish, loving devotion to the God who lavished us with extravagant grace.

Wordsworth put it well when he wrote:

> *Give all thou canst;*
> *High Heaven rejects the lore*
> *Of nicely calculated less or more.*
>   (Inside Kings College Chapel, Cambridge)

But famous preacher poet and one-time Dean of St. Paul's London, John Donne, put it even better when he wrote:

> *I am two fools I know,*
> *One for loving*
> *And for saying so*
> *In whining poetry.*

Ah, Mary, you know what he meant! And so do you, Mary Magdalene. And so do we when by chance we step on an elevator to smell a perfume that is sacramental. A perfume that takes us back into the grace and joy and acceptance of dinners and love and the feelings of extravagant giving.

And, oh, yes, you can be sure the poor will benefit.

Prayer

O Eternal God, who has brought us into this fair world of sight and sense, a world of sound and sensuous delights of food and wine, with textures and fragrances and tastes nearly infinite in number, we praise and adore you for the mysterious complexities of our living and experiencing. Day by day we behold the world with amazement, and night by night we gaze into your glories in the heavens and in the eyes of our beloved.

We come into this sacred time and place to feast again upon the pleasures of your grace. Your eternal words come to us as soothing sounds to our spiritual mind, and your reassuring truths are life-sustaining food for our sometimes famished soul.

As we are sustained day by day with physical food, so day by day we would be sustained with your spiritual food. Help us now to open our minds and hearts to receive spiritual nourishment you have for us out of your holy Word. If we have feasted upon the things of this world only to come away hungry, help us today and always to feast upon your everlasting truths and thus be deeply satisfied.

We pray for our children and grandchildren, whether here or far away, that they might be nurtured on your truth and sustained by your grace. We pray for all those who have been in bondage to ignorance and superstition, shackled by traditions, and inhibited by fear. Grant them the enlightenment of your truth and the liberation of your grace. So may we all as a human race come together in a great spiritual banquet of understanding and peace. Through Jesus Christ our Lord. Amen.

8. The Dinner Party Not To Miss

And the master said to the servant, "Go out and compel people to come in, that my house may be filled. For I tell you, none of those men who were invited shall taste my banquet." — Luke 14:23-24

Have you received any good invitations lately? I certainly have, as has my wife. People have been most gracious to invite my wife and me to lunch or dinner and other social occasions. And once when my wife was away in Norway and Sweden, people had worried I might waste away without her excellent cooking. Consequently, I was the fortunate recipient of many invitations to lunch and dinner.

Only recently I was at a wedding reception where sumptuous food was served. For example, we had scallops and bacon, pizza bagels, mozzarella sticks, baked stuffed clams, clams casino, crab claws, pork, beef, and lamb on skewer, and stuffed mushrooms.

There also were beef and shrimp Chinese style, rigatoni and broccoli, fusilli primavera, chicken francais, calamari, roast rack of lamb, baked Virginia ham, and fruit and cheese board. We also had vodka and caviar, poached lobsters, shrimp, deviled eggs, and smoked salmon. Those were only the appetizers. After that we sat down to a several course dinner. It was a dinner party not to miss.

How about you? Have you been invited out to lunch or brunch, or to a good dinner party? Has anyone suggested you join their yacht or country club? How about a prestigious business or professional group? Have they been knocking at your door? Any invitations to join a service club, or serve on a board, or run for office? It is important to accept the right invitations.

It is interesting to note how many invitations there are in the Bible, especially invitations to feasts, banquets, and dinner parties. From the very beginning God has invited humankind to eat, suggesting to Adam and Eve they enjoy all the fruit and produce of the

Garden of Eden, save one. Throughout the history of Israel, the Hebrews are invited to religious feasts and banquets and occasions for covenant renewal.

The prophet Isaiah speaks for the Lord when he utters the great invitation:

> *Ho, everyone who thirsts,*
> *come to the waters;*
> *And he who has no money,*
> *come, buy and eat!*
> *Come, buy wine and milk*
> *without money and without price.*
>
> *Why do you spend your money for*
> *that which is not bread,*
> *And your labor for that which*
> *does not satisfy?* — Isaiah 55:1-2

And in the New Testament, we have one invitation after another. "Come, follow me," says Jesus, "and I will make you fishers of men." And again, "Come unto me all ye that labor and are heavy laden and I will give you rest." And again, "Behold, I stand at the door and knock, if anyone hears my voice and opens the door, I will come in to him and eat with him and he with me."

Most of all, Jesus issues invitations to the Kingdom of God, using the imagery of dinner parties, banquets, and feasts. Not only that, he himself regularly accepted invitations to dinner parties. Remember when he went to dine with Levi, the customs collector and with Zacchaeus, the tax collector. Another time, he was with Simon the Pharisee, where the prostitute washed his feet with her tears and dried them with her hair. How does that scene strike you in light of the Jim Bakker and Jimmy Swaggart scandals?

The truth is, many thought Jesus could not possibly be religious while enjoying so many dinner parties with such a questionable crowd of tax collectors, prostitutes, and social outcasts. Many thought religion was a much more solemn affair and that a religious man should be a borderline anorexic with at least a mild case of dyspepsia. For some, religion was too serious a matter for anything but perpetual fasting and sullen withdrawal from laughter and good times.

To such persons, John the Baptist, with his diet of wild honey and locusts, his wardrobe of camel's hair coat and leather girdle, his fierce eyes and steadfast refusal to leave the wilderness to accept compromising dinner invitations — to such persons judgmental John was the ideal, almost. And today, exercise buffs, dieters, health food faddists, and borderline anorexics hail John as a patron saint. Look closely and you will see no cellulite or heart disease or any other of the ailments of overstuffed civilization in John.

For those reasons, and countless others, I have always preferred Jesus over John. Sure, Jesus had his times in the wilderness when fasting was in order. And we need those times too. But most often he was with people attending parties, dinners, and banquets. His first recorded miracle was at the wedding feast in Cana of Galilee where he turned water into wine — estate bottled, proprietor's premium reserve red wine, vintage, 5 A.D.!

Invitations to dinner parties for Jesus? Yes, lots of them. Good food and wine? Yes, plenty of it. Jokes and stories and laughter? To be sure. No wonder then Jesus used the imagery of banquets and feasts and dinner parties to describe the Kingdom of God. It is to be like that, a party of good food and drink brimming over with happiness and joy. Heaven itself is described as a gigantic family reunion where we live joyfully with our Lord and those loved long since and lost a while.

And yet, Jesus had trouble getting people to accept invitations to the Kingdom. He said some of God's messengers piped to you and you did not dance, others wailed and you would not wail. John the Baptist came eating no bread and drinking no wine in an effort to call people into the Kingdom and they accused him of having a demon or being a little crazy. "I come," says Jesus, "eating and drinking and attending dinner parties, and you accuse me of being glutton and drunkard, a friend of tax collectors and sinners" (Luke 7:31-35). Two opposite approaches and still people did not know how to accept the right invitation.

How about us? Do we have that wisdom? Do we want to be included in the great banquet of the Kingdom? What keeps us from it? Jesus' story gives the clues.

I.

The first man in Jesus' story who was invited to the Kingdom banquet excused himself saying he had bought some property and had to go and see it.

This man symbolized those who put business and profession and money ahead of the Kingdom of God. Indeed, it can symbolize those who think the Kingdom of God *is* success in business or profession.

And let us make no mistake about it. Many of us identify with him, for we often agree with Charles Wilson, former head of General Motors, who said that the business of America is business.

The influential sociologist, C. Wright Mills, once observed astutely: "Of all the possible values of human society, one and only one is truly sovereign, truly universal, truly sound, truly and completely acceptable goal of man in America. That goal is money, and let there be no sour grapes about it from the losers" (*The Power Elite*, p. 164).

And those of us who have tasted the sweet fruits of financial success know precisely what he means. We know well the deep satisfaction of achieving, of getting out ahead of the crowd, and of having the money to buy almost everything we want. Many of us will work long hours even to the neglect of family and health to reach our goals of financial success. The pressure and competition are very real, but they provide an even greater incentive to achieve the rewards of the good life and the admiration of our peers.

So why shouldn't this man look after his investments? Business first, other matters second, right? After all, where would the church be without the money we give from our businesses? Financial success is the first order of the day. We can pick up religion later on once we are established and secure, can we not?

Possibly, but like the man who built bigger and bigger barns, it may be too late. Like him, we may say, soul, take thine ease, you have enough to be secure for years, not knowing our soul may be required of us this very night. Many young men fall by the way with heart attacks before they achieve success. Women still outlive men by several years, but their early death rate is picking up. And yet many delay the first question of life until the last, namely, "How is it with your soul?" Have you accepted Christ's invitation to the eternal Kingdom?

Oh, to be sure, Christ is making no case for failure in the world. Instead, he is making a case for success in the Kingdom of God. Our Lord is not against making money. Instead he warns against using money as an immortality symbol as Ernest Becker suggests in his book *The Denial of Death*. It is difficult to buy eternal life with temporal mammon.

After all, if we had all the money we wanted, what would we do then? Eat, drink, take our ease? Yes. Ask with songstress Peggy Lee, "Is that all there is?" Yes. Begin to wonder about life's meaning and purpose, about death and judgment and life eternal? Hopefully. And Jesus is telling us the last question is really the first. Seek *first* the Kingdom of God, and then these things, the necessities of life, will be added unto you from the proper perspective.

II.

In Jesus' story, the second man invited to the Kingdom banquet turned down his invitation, saying he had bought five yoke of oxen and had to go examine them.

In that time, five yoke of oxen symbolized power. Here was a man who had the wherewithal to get things done. He represents the thinking of many that power and money are two of the most important matters of life. Power, the ability to make things happen, is what it is all about.

For some years now, power has been located not only in business, but in politics. In the 1960s and 1970s many young people flocked to Washington to be an active part of the political bureaucracy and power structure. From local to state to national, politics was perceived to be where the action was.

Many ministerial students of my generation avoided the local church like the plague. They thought it an anemic, bourgeois institution where the minister was a political eunuch. In the eyes of the anti-institutional generation, the church was the anemic, powerless chaplain of the American Way where the dull consoled the dull and the bland led the bland. No wonder the young left it in droves. They wanted to be where the action was, and that often meant politics.

Let us not be like those who, suffering from failure of nerve as are many Americans, believe religion has nothing to do with power. The contrary. It is precisely power with which it has to do. After all, if God is all-powerful, and if religion has to do with God, how can it avoid dealing with questions of power? The Protestant Church has been especially naive and innocuous in this area and has been pushed for years to the periphery of power. Many Protestants have confused humility with spinelessness and kindness with weakness. One of the kindest things we can do for church and society is not to *withdraw* from the centers of power, but to use power wisely in kindly, helpful ways.

Therefore, the issue in Jesus' story is not power as such, but rather the true location of power and its proper use. Just where is it we find power? In politics? Yes, but it is temporal, sometimes fickle or corrupt and extremely changeable. In the military? Yes, to be sure, but now it is so out of control, so threatening, so terrifying, so destructive, that we are rendered relatively powerless in our fear of annihilating civilization.

Is there power in money, prestige, fame, knowledge? To be sure. But the real power, the real *dynamis*, or dynamite, or dynamo, the real source of life is in God in whom we live and move and have our being. It was at another dinner party that Jesus told his disciples they are not to use their power to exploit, oppress, and lord it over others. Instead, they were to use their power as God uses his — responsibly, faithfully, honorably, lovingly, justly, and tenderly to serve the needs of our fellows rather than to rip them off.

All human power is derivative and is, in the end, illusory. Power belongs to God, says the Bible repeatedly. To place our ultimate confidence in man's power is a poor bargain, says Jesus. Will you not accept the invitation to participate in the true power of God?

III.

The third man in the story rejects the invitation to the Kingdom banquet to attend to his marriage and family. One wag has it that he didn't come because his wife wouldn't let him out of the house.

According to Jewish custom, a newly married man was excluded from military service and other social obligations during the first year of marriage. That was rightly regarded as an important time of adjustment and enjoyment.

With all the stress today on marriage and family, who would want to take anyone away from his home? We could rightly argue that men and women are too much away from each other and that that is part of the problem. Some people say that is why they don't come to church. Sunday is the only time they have to be together, so they ski, hunt, boat, fish, play tennis or golf, dine or loaf, or go to the cottage on Sunday. Church interferes with their rare opportunities for togetherness, they say.

However, those of us who own boats and cottages know there is a sense in which they own us. One time a lady of a Minneapolis church came up to me after church and said, "Reverend Fetty, you're going to see a lot more of us on Sundays. We've sold our cottage and we're finally free on weekends!" Yes, finally free!

Families are given high value in God's order of things, but couples and families can close in on themselves, becoming selfish and suffocating, building an insulated paradise for two or ten. Families can become clannish, snobbish, insular without opening up to the wider realities of God's Kingdom. Jesus knew that when he said that a man who loved family more than God was not worthy of the Kingdom. God alone is worthy of worship. The family, no matter how dear, is not. The Kingdom and church call the family away from selfishness and suffocating self-centeredness into the larger cause.

IV.

There is reason to believe this great story of Jesus was based on a Jewish Talmudic story where a certain man, Bar Ma'jan, a rich tax collector, held a dinner party. Remember that tax collectors were outcasts because they were collaborationists and agents of the hated Romans. So Bar Ma'jan held a large feast, hoping thereby to be accepted by insiders of higher society. But they agreed together to refuse his invitation and deny him acceptance. So Bar Ma'jan invited the poor to come so the food would not be wasted.

Consider Jesus. He was not a tax collector or hated Roman collaborationist, but he was an outsider. He was from Nazareth, out of which nothing good comes, said the Jerusalem snobs. Jesus came without pedigree, without money, without credentials and connections, and entered into the religious capital and offered the feast of the Kingdom of God to insider Israelites. But they all agreed together to reject him and not to allow him to be an accepted leader among them or a representative of God's Kingdom.

Therefore, Jesus the outsider, who is rejected by insiders, invites all the outsiders into the Kingdom and they gladly accept, surprised and overjoyed that they are included.

Thus, Gentiles, publicans, prostitutes, and sinners go into the Kingdom before the socially and religiously elite. God's grace transcends all the boundaries of social registers, club lists, religious creeds and dogmas, denominations and hierarchies. The religiously unscrupulous and the socially inept and unsophisticated, the bag ladies, street people, and day laborers are included, whereas often the snobbish, the elite, and the religiously narrow and exclusive are excluded.

Jesus' invitation is refused by many of the successful, the powerful, and those well-placed in well-connected families. They are too busy, too preoccupied, too content that they are insiders to take seriously the message of the Kingdom. Mildly contemptuous of the church, they see religion as somewhat beneath them. At best it is a convenience for baptisms and confirmations, weddings and funerals.

We are to remember that we are outsiders to some group no matter how much we think ourselves the insiders. Some businessmen and environmentalists are outsiders to one another, as are fundamentalists and liberals, pro-abortion and anti-abortion people, Republicans and Democrats, old, stuffy money and fluffy, new money, the big line of credit and the poor credit risks, sociologists and the middle class, blacks and Hispanics, feminists and male chauvinists, and on and on.

That is why this great parable is such good news for it invites *all* of us — insiders and outsiders — into the great banquet feast of the Kingdom of God. This *is* the *right* invitation. We send our regrets at our peril. But today we celebrate the fact that many of us have accepted the invitation. This is the dinner party not to miss. You are invited. Are you coming?

Prayer

Almighty God, Maker of the world and our Maker, before whom the morning stars sing together and the sons of God shout for joy, praise be to you for the glory of the universe and the wonder of the world. Today in your presence we would remove any spiritual cataracts or any moral glaucoma which would prevent us from beholding you in your glory and majesty. Praise be to you, Almighty God. All the world awakens to you as the earth to the morning sun.

Look upon us now in your mercy as we approach you with confession and request. See us in the wrong use of our need to belong. You have made us for community. You have designed us to find ourselves in our relationships with others.

But we confess to you how often we have joined ourselves to the wrong person or group. As the Bible says, bad companions corrupt good morals. With this group or that, our judgment and morals have been corrupted in the anxiety of loneliness. In the uncertainty of selfhood, we have attached ourselves to those whom we should have avoided. Forgive us, O God, and open doors for new and healthier relationships, we pray.

We pray especially for our young people. Vibrant, energetic, and anxious to belong, they often find themselves in the wrong crowd. Pressured by high achiever parents and enticed to conform to their peers, our young are lured to alcohol and drugs and wrong use of sex. O Lord our God, how earnestly we pray for your help in bringing them to yourself, and to the kind of group that honors you and your principles. Bless all groups, especially the Church, who in your name reach out to our young.

And for our adults we pray discernment. Some of us have gotten into patterns of conduct and ways of behavior which are displeasing to you. In our search for love and understanding, in our desire to be included and to belong, we sometimes have surrendered our deeper convictions and higher moral standards. Help us be more responsive to the nudgings of your Spirit rather than always being anxious to be in step with the spirit of the times.

Bless the Church that it might be renewed with the sense of divine community. Help us to realize anew our oneness with you and with the Church of the ages. Grant that our first aim shall be always to have our name written in the Book of Life, that it might ever be said that we belong to you forever. Through Jesus Christ our Lord. Amen.

9. Parable Of The Marriage Feast

For many are called, but few are chosen.
— Matthew 22:14

Jesus had quite a lot to say about banquets, dinner parties, and marriage feasts. Unlike the somewhat antisocial, ascetic John the Baptist, who spent his life in the wilderness disdaining the niceties of culture, Jesus frequently could be found on the banquet circuit.

And he wasn't too choosy as to whose banquet it was. It could be the wedding feast at Cana where he changed water into really good wine. It could be a more quiet dinner party with Mary, Martha, and Lazarus. Or it could be with Zacchaeus, the converted swindler, or Levi, the changed tax collector. Simon, the self-righteous Pharisee, entertained him as did countless others.

Jesus probably attended fellowship suppers and potluck synagogue dinners. He may have shown up for graduation parties. Whatever the case, he knew well the feast and banquet circuit — so much so he was accused of being a glutton and winebibber. He wasn't, of course. But he did attend a lot of parties.

So Jesus knew about banquets, dinner parties, and marriage feasts — big ones, small ones, important ones, unimportant ones, religious ones, and some not so religious. He could have written a book about banquet etiquette. More importantly, he used his experience of banquets and feasts to illustrate the Kingdom of God.

Our text speaks of a marriage feast and the guests who did not honor their invitation and the guests who did. This parable of the marriage feast is told to illustrate the Kingdom of God and our relationship with it.

The parable is told to illustrate at least three things about the Kingdom. It is impending, important, and inclusive.

I.

The Kingdom of God is *impending*. It is breaking in here and now. It is not just some far off distant event. It is at hand, always at hand, with its urgency and demand.

Says Joseph Alexander:

> *There is a time, we know not when,*
> *A point we know not where*
> *That marks the destiny of men,*
> *For glory or despair.*
>
> *There is a line, by us unseen,*
> *That crosses every path;*
> *That hidden boundary between*
> *God's patience and his wrath.*

There is a time, a line that determines our destiny. It is the occasion of our invitation to the banquet of the Kingdom of God. It is the time of the summons of God to the new duties of the new time of history. It is the moment of putting our hand to the plow and not looking back.

Yet, that is often our failing — looking back into the past, reaching back for that idyllic time when all seemed peace and fulfillment, triumph and completion. When was it in your life? Graduation day from high school or college? Was it the winning touchdown in the last minutes of your high school football career? Your starring role in music or drama?

While the past is important, we sometimes look back into it so much we get lost in it. That is nostalgia and sentimentality. That will never do for the Kingdom of God. The Kingdom is impending, urging us to come to the Lord's banquet, the marriage feast, to celebrate the Kingdom's cause. It urges us to accept the invitation now. It places new opportunities and challenges before us. Put your hand to the plow and don't look back.

Some time ago I was having breakfast in a restaurant. There was a shortage of tables, so the hostess asked if a man could join me. I agreed. As our conversation moved along, he discovered I was a minister. Almost immediately he shifted gears and began to tell me about his religious, born-again experience that had happened forty or fifty years ago.

But as he continued at great length I wanted to ask him, but what have you done about the Kingdom of God since that important experience? Hasn't Christ called you to put your hand to some new plow? What have you done to better the Church? How have you helped resolve the huge social problems of our time? Do you give generously to the Church? What kind of relationship have you developed with your family?

Here was a man who saw the Kingdom of God only as past event. He believed the fullness of time occurred only with his spiritual rebirth, rather than with his growth and the developed decisions of maturity. Here was a man physically well dressed, attired in spiritual diapers. He could eat physical bacon but needed spiritual milk. He regarded the spiritual birth trauma as the normative spiritual experience rather than growth and maturity

But the time of Christ's feast is now, the eternal now, that is forever confronting us, and issuing us a new invitation to God's Kingdom. We are not to lament with A. E. Houseman who wrote:

And how am I to face the odds
Of man's bedevilment and God's?
I, a stranger and afraid
In a world I never made.

True, the times are full of difficulty and stress. It is tempting to escape back into the memories of high school when college is staring us in the face. Often we would rather rest on some past triumph than confront a future challenge. But the Kingdom of God is impending and summons us to faith and courage.

Near the center of England, in the village of Stanton-Harold, there is an inscription in a small chapel which reads:

In the year 1653
  When all things sacred were
  throughout the nation
Either demolished or profaned

> *Sir Robert Shirley, Baronet*
> *founded this church*
> *Whose singular praise it is*
> *to have done the best things*
> *In the worst of times, and*
> *Hoped them in the most calamitous.*

Whether it be the best of times, or the worst of times, the invitation to God's Kingdom is impending. Like Sir Robert Shirley, let us accept in faith and hope.

II.

Secondly, the Kingdom of God is *important*. The invitation to this marriage feast to the Kingdom is not to be overlooked or rejected. No other activity should take precedence. No other affair or affection should assume more importance. Yet to many of the people in this parable, other things were more important than the Feast of the Kingdom.

In this story, when the servants of the king went out to invite the honored guests to the feast, they made light of it and went off, one to his farm, another to his business, and others even treated the servants violently.

Historically, Jesus probably was referring to the Jews who refused the invitation to the king's marriage feast for his son. God most likely is the King. Jesus is his son, and the servants of God are the prophets and messengers of God sent to his people throughout the ages. Like any king, God invited the nobility to his feast. And in that day and setting, the Jews represented the religious nobility. But, even though they represented the religious establishment and aristocracy, they were too busy to come. They had more important things to do than respond to the invitation.

Today, many of us church-types represent that religious nobility. We have had the privilege of the knowledge of God's law and love. We have benefited from the great teachings and noble principles and high ethical standards. And yet when the invitation arrives for God's feast, we are too busy. We claim to have more important things to do.

The people in the parable were preoccupied with property and business. We know these people well. They are those pre-occupied with business or profession. They are the up-and-coming salesmen who stop at nothing to make a dollar. They are the ambitious junior executives, the compulsive laborers, the work-ethic dominated farmers, the over-zealous lawyers, the aspiring actresses who compromise everything for success, the power-prone, status-conscious professors, the unteachable teachers, the smother-mothers whose tyranny is thinly disguised as maternity.

Both the challenge and the delight of the Kingdom's importance is that it will call us to tasks in which our own egos will be lost in exhilarating service. The Kingdom is so much more vast than our talents, so much greater than our limited potential. After we have been sitting at the banquets of forced gaiety prepared by our own wealth and wisdom, we soon find that our bread doesn't satisfy and that our wine is flat and stale, leaving a bitter aftertaste. Maybe then we will see the importance of God's invitation to his feast.

Those of us in the religious establishment sometimes do not understand the importance of God's invitation because we confuse the Kingdom with institutionalism. But as Archbishop William Temple was fond of saying, "God is not primarily interested in religion." Instead he is interested in a new people who sense a new beginning, a new age, a new humankind. He is seeking those persons who see that the Kingdom of God has arrived in history and who are ready to respond to its importance.

But religious establishment people often suffer from Parkinson's Law about institutions. One of his laws says that work expands to fill the time available for its completion. He suggests the number of institutional workers and the quantity of work are not related to each other at all. Or as Senator Everett Dirkson once said, many institutions are like the rocking chair: it gives you a sense of motion without any sense of danger.

How easy it is for us to become like the people in the parable. We first possess our possessions and then they possess us. We build our institutions to serve us, and then we find ourselves serving them.

Life gets inverted, and we miss the important invitation to the impending Kingdom of God, always arriving for those ready to receive it. Many are called, but few are chosen. Many are issued invitations, but few respond because they think they have more important things to do.

III.

Thirdly, not only is the Kingdom impending and important, it is *inclusive*.

Many in Jesus' time thought the Kingdom was only for a select few — for the religiously correct, the piously perfect, the cultured insiders — in short, for Pharisees. Yet, it is precisely these people who refuse the invitation to the marriage feast of God's Son. They are preoccupied with businesses, careers, families, and even with religious institutionalism. They thought the Kingdom was their possession, available to them like a good country club when they wanted to use it.

Regrettably, the story is repeated again and again in Christian history. Some groups identify their particular group with the Kingdom to the exclusion of others. A Boston church, cultured and sophisticated, singing only the finest of music, looks down its nose at the gospel singing of a Southern Baptist church in Arkansas. The Baptist Church returns the favor by pointing out the absence of commitment and personal faith of the Boston church.

Some liberal churches smile bemusedly at the antics of some evangelicals, while evangelicals point knowingly at the pallid countenance and spiritual anemia of many liberal churches. Well-educated congregations are shocked at the poor taste of Bible-quoting conservatives and fundamentalists, while conservatives and fundamentalists point knowingly at the biblical and theological ignorance of many well-educated Christians.

But notice what happened in this parable: those least likely to be invited were sought out by God's servants and they accepted. From the ghettoes, the slums, the highways and byways; from saloons, divorce courts, government halls, cocktail lounges, and broken homes they came. Even ex-convicts arrived and outcasts came.

Young, old, and middle-aged came. Rich and poor arrived, trusting neither in their poverty nor their wealth, but in the grace of God.

But there is this warning. Inclusiveness in the Kingdom of God is not to be taken for granted. Remember the conclusion of the parable. One man came but did not dress properly. He was glad to be invited, but imposed upon the graciousness of his host by refusing to wear the wedding attire provided for him. Consequently the king threw him out of the feast. Any person so ungrateful and disrespectful of his high privilege did not deserve to remain. When the Kingdom is taken for granted it is taken away and given to others.

Could it be the Western world has become like the guest without a proper garment? Alexander Solzhenitsyn, speaking some time ago at a Harvard commencement, chastised the West for its "psychological weakness," "spiritual exhaustion," and lack of "civil courage." "No weapons, no matter how powerful, can help the West until it overcomes its lack of will power," said the Nobel prize-winning, exiled Russian Christian.

The real crisis of our time is not the confrontation between East and West, but materialism, humanism, and lack of spiritual life throughout the world. "We have placed too much hope in political and social reforms, only to find out that we were being deprived of our most precious possession, our spiritual life." Solzhenitsyn continued to say that the West was debilitated by the "dream of the status quo ... a symptom of a society which has come to the end of its development."

He warned that the West may become less and less a model for the world to follow. Referring to hardships faced by Eastern Europeans and Russians, he said, "Through intense suffering our country (Russia) has now achieved a spiritual development of such intensity that the Western system in its present state of spiritual exhaustion does not look attractive."

Our country may be like the guest of the marriage feast without the proper garment — the garment of gratitude, humility, and spiritual depth. We may have come to take the Kingdom for granted.

It may well be the East German Christian student who used to give up a college education and professional career because of his

Christian faith, may know much more about the Kingdom than the American student who assumes college and career and readily gives up his faith and church or takes them for granted.

It may well be the oppressed and deprived peoples of the world may know the importance of the Kingdom more than those of us affluent, satiated with good things and nonchalant about the important values of faith and freedom.

The Kingdom is inclusive, but those without the proper garments of faith, humility, and gratitude may well be thrown out. Mr. Solzhenitsyn continued, "If the world has not come to its end, it has approached a major turn in history, equal in importance to the turn from the Middle Ages to the Renaissance. It will exact from us a spiritual upsurge; we shall have to rise to a new height of vision. This ascension will be similar to climbing onto the next anthropologic stage. No one on earth has any other way left but upward" (Quotes from *Christian Science Monitor*, June 9, 1978, p. 3).

Solzhenitsyn's warning is loud and clear. Let us not presume upon God or take the Kingdom for granted. Let us wear the proper garments of gratitude and humility.

We gather around the Communion table celebrating the inclusiveness of God's Kingdom. We eat and drink at the feast in anticipation of a new age, a new day, and finally in anticipation of the great heavenly feast, the marriage supper of Christ and his Church. Christ is the Lamb of God. And it is by his blood, by his life, that the church has life and love and forgiveness.

There is no more important feast in the world, for it always reminds us that God's Kingdom is impending, important, and inclusive.

Prayer

Loving Father, Creator of all that is, source of power and love, who takes more delight in the birth of a child than in the birth of a galaxy; and who takes more pride in the spiritual radiance upon a man's face than in the light of a thousand suns; we worship you and adore you. You have brought us forth from the dust of the earth and given us your life. And you have brought us forth once again from the ruins and dust of our guilt and failures to give us new life, to recreate us to enable us to begin again. We praise you and give you thanks. Receive us then as we approach your throne of glory.

We confess our frequent need of a new vision to things; thus we approach you for the broader, higher perspective. We too often are lowland people, trudging along in the valleys of our discontent, contained by the lofty hills and mountain ranges about us. Or, we have been too long dwellers on the plains where life has become flat and dull. And though we can see for miles, it is more of the same.

We pray, Loving Father, maker of the mountains, that you will lure us again to the higher perspective and nobler vision. If we have gone along in a rut and resigned ourselves to a dreary sameness day after day, bring us again at least to the foothills of life, where we may get a fresh glimpse of a new way. If we have let ourselves become flat and boring, lure us on like westward pioneers to the mountains which give exhilaration to men's souls. Release us from spiritual doldrums — from self-pity and defeatism, from depression and a sense of futility. Help us see again the person we might become and fortify our souls for the new adventure.

We beseech your mercy and pity for the world. Grant by your Spirit a new sense of integrity among world leaders. Help us find ways to deal with terrorism. Save us from lusting after the wild war music so enticing to some ears. In a world nearly floating in gunpowder and nuclear bombs, quiet the raging impulses of all desperate peoples that this fair planet be not maimed and destroyed. Oh, how we pray for a new day of peace in the world.

Be pleased to visit your Church with a new spirit. If we have succumbed too much to the present age; if our hearts have hardened and our energies waned; visit us again with a new understanding of our Lord Christ who is forever calling us onward to the new day. Bless the Church for its tasks in your Kingdom. Through Jesus Christ our Lord. Amen.

10. The Great Invitation

For many are called, but few are chosen.
— Matthew 22:14 (RSV)

Not long ago a woman told me of her experiences when she and her husband received an invitation to dine with the President at the White House. They cancelled all other engagements, went to Washington at their own expense, and booked in at one of the better hotels. She continued her plans for the Presidential dinner by having her hair done just right. She bought an expensive new dress, bathed for a long time, applied the best perfume, adorned herself with her finest jewelry, and finally, after days of preparation, actually went to the dinner in style. And she and her husband loved every minute of it. They had been included and accepted at the dinner table of the free world's most powerful man.

A man once was a candidate for a high executive position with a large corporation. The interview process had proceeded along its various stages. Now the candidate and his wife were invited to a dinner party with the President, Chairman of the Board, and leading board members. Knowing well the significance of the occasion, the man bought a new suit and his wife shopped several days to find just the right dress. Her hair and nails were faultless, her make-up and jewelry stunning, yet tasteful. She thoroughly educated herself on corporate policy and current affairs. The big night came and they were a smash. They passed with flying colors. Her husband got the job and they were initiated into the rewards, perquisites, and inside mysteries of our nation's executive elite.

A doctor, a specialist, moved into town, took up residence in an exclusive neighborhood, associated himself with a medical group, and attached himself to a hospital. His senior partner invited him to a dinner party which included the head of the medical staff and a few key internists from whom they received many referrals. The doctor and his wife cancelled other plans, prepared themselves with new suit and dress, groomed themselves thoroughly, briefed themselves on pertinent information regarding the people attending the dinner. They even familiarized themselves with the history of the hospital and the city and took great pains to learn discreetly the current political battles going on in the medical community. They were a big hit and they were on their way in a very successful medical career.

A leading family in the community, well-to-do and highly respected, had an only son who was to be married. So the family sent out invitations to their relatives and friends; to their business associates, lawyers, doctors; to their golf and bridge partners, to their college buddies and poker cronies, and even to their minister. Noting the importance of the invitation, everyone came, except for one man who stayed home to watch the World Series. First things first!

Upon seeing how well people respond to important dinner parties that are keys to acceptance and success, God himself decided to throw a big party for his son who was to be married. He spent a long time getting things ready. He decided to build a new banquet hall and grow all the food himself so everything would be fresh and just right. God didn't just send invitations. He had messengers deliver them personally. And each messenger delivered the invitation in his own unique style. Some wrote exquisite poetry. Some acted it out or delivered a dramatic speech. Others even wrote beautiful music. And according to God's customs in the Near East, he sent the messengers again to remind everyone that the time had arrived. Everything was perfectly prepared. Come to the big dinner party.

God was really excited, because contrary to popular opinion with some so-called godly people, God really enjoys a good time. He knew well that all work and no play makes even God a dull boy. For example, he really thought it unfortunate if a wedding feast should run out of wine and have to resort to plain old water. If you are going to have a party, might as well kill the fatted calf. After all, what are you saving it for?

So the big day arrived. The chefs had been working for a long time in the kitchen. God's big house was absolutely beautiful — exquisite, in fact, with delicate fragrances of every conceivable flower and alive with the delicate songs of the finest birds. God made a big fire in the fireplace and lighted the candles himself.

The table was beautifully set with diamond crystal, goldware, and china of pearl. He had live dinner music and even provided some cigars he had sneaked out of Cuba before Castro smoked them all.

God had been a little bit worried as to whether he would have everything ready on time, because he kept thinking up new things to add to the party to make it a grand affair. He truly wanted it to be a memorable occasion, one where people truly would be happy and satisfied. He wanted it to be something they would remember the rest of their lives.

Anyhow, despite his worries, everything was ready. So he sent his messengers on their way to invite his closest friends and associates, those he had done business with most often, to come, because the feast was ready and he was waiting and his son was excited. In fact, most of his invited guests were wholesalers, distributors, and retailers of his product. Some were in marketing or public relations. Some were manufacturers' representatives. Others were in the education and entertainment ends of the business. But all were, for the most part, connected in one way or another with one of his biggest corporations. And frankly, all had done quite nicely with his product.

You can imagine, therefore, how stunned God was when his messengers came back and said that his guests had turned him down, sending their regrets that they were unable to attend. God couldn't believe his ears. Surely there must be a mix-up. Perhaps the communication was garbled or people just didn't get the date and time right. Possibly his invited guests didn't recognize the messengers as there is some turnover in his business. At any rate, he had been planning this wedding party for a long time and was looking forward to a really good time.

So, giving his guests the benefit of the doubt, he sent a higher echelon of advisors to tell his guests that the party was ready, that it was time to come. Surely his distributors, wholesalers, and retailers and all the others associated with his corporation would recognize these well known messengers, some of whom even wrote some new poetry and music and invitation speeches.

But when the messengers returned God was astounded at their report. All the people made excuses, even made light of the invitation. Some said they had just made a big real estate deal and couldn't leave right at that time. Others claimed they were opening up a whole new territory for business and really couldn't be away that day. Others were even angry with God for meddling in their lives and affairs and beat up God's messengers so God would be sure to get the message. They even killed one of God's top advisors to show him they were independent and really didn't need him.

Now God was a nice guy and all that, but he wasn't a patsy. Who did those people think they were? He knew how people tend to become arrogant and snobbish when they are successful. He had seen some of his leading wholesalers become ungrateful and insolent with him. Some of his retailers even forgot where they got their product in the first place. Some of the advertising people started to believe they created both the product and the need for it. And not a few in the business believed they could produce the product themselves if they had to. It was obvious now that outright rebellion had set in and that these people believed they could be successful and have their good life without God.

Enough is enough. So God sent his lawyers and withdrew all the franchises, seized all his property, and publicly denounced these arrogant and rebellious representatives. Of course they had some product left over and continued to sell it. But God had turned off their main pipeline and soon they would be out of business. God knows what every good businessman knows — that in the last analysis religion must be run like a business.

It was a funny thing that happened, and, to tell you the truth, God had seen it happen before. He chooses some people, provides them with a good education in some of his best schools, gives them some of the best medical care in some of his hospitals, acquaints them with some of his best music, literature, and art, and gives them some of the world's best political concepts, and then sets them up in business.

And are the people grateful? For a while, yes. But you know how it is. They get absorbed in their own thing. They get some notoriety and some money. They hear the praise of men and the accolades of their subordinates and even start to believe their own press releases. They begin to take for granted their resources and overestimate their abilities. Soon they regard themselves as self-made men and throw themselves headlong into the race to the top.

In fact, God was reminded of the riverboat captain on the Mississippi who was carrying a cargo of meat from New Orleans to Memphis. Another boat tried to pass him and the race was on. He ordered full steam ahead, but it was not enough to pull ahead of the other boat.

So he ordered them to throw some of the fat of the meat into the fire, and that gave an added thrust. So he had them throw on more and more meat and he pulled ahead arriving in Memphis with whistles blowing and flags flying. But when the merchants came for their meat, they found it had been burned up in the race. So it will be with these people who burn out their souls to win the race. They think they save their lives, but really they lose them because when the race is over they end up empty handed.

Well, back to our story. Two things God could not stand were arrogance and ingratitude. After he had spent all that time setting his people up in business, after he had virtually assured them of success and the good life, after he had patiently helped them through crises and over problems, after all that, to have them snub him was just too much. He knew that people often snub the invitations of social climbers and the newly rich as a put-down, but to go so far as to snub him was just too much. So he pulled their plug. They had it coming. He might be merciful, but he was no fool. So they were out.

But God was determined to have a great wedding feast and dinner party for his son. So he sent his messengers out again to people he had never seriously invited before. Some had a lot of potential but were not too well educated. Others were talented but not well trained. Still others had never before really been in business, nor had they ever been in such exclusive, high-quality surroundings.

Not only did he invite the masses of disadvantaged people to the feast. He decided to offer them franchises in his business. True, they might not be as well qualified initially, but he would work with them and they would grow. True, they were not as experienced as the others, but that would come. Yes, it might take a while to get the production lines and sales force going again. But he would do it, because God liked to do business. He liked parties and good times. But even God, who owns just about everything, is not a playboy. He likes to work hard and expects his subordinates to do the same.

In fact, it could be said that God almost had the Protestant work ethic, even though he noted lately that Catholics seemed to have more of the Protestant work ethic than Protestants. To tell the truth, he was beginning to think Protestants were a bit slovenly and unreliable. In America, for example, where production is so poor, there is a Protestant majority. So they must be responsible for some of the shoddy workmanship and inferior production.

At any rate, both God and the Protestants and Catholics put aside their work for a while (such as it was), and had a great time at the party. It was absolutely wonderful. The food was out of this world. The music and entertainment were heavenly. And the feeling — well, the feeling was unlike anything the people had experienced before. In fact, in some ways, the feeling was even new to God. He loved it and decided then and there that from now on, he would open up his parties to anyone who wanted to come. He would send out a general invitation and those who accepted would be included. More than that, he also decided he would open up his business franchises to anyone who wanted to try. What a party it was. What a feast. What a wonderful new beginning for everyone, including God.

However, the celebration was not without its problems. As the party was going at full tilt, God noticed someone who hadn't dressed properly for the occasion. Now God had declared that this was to be a coat and tie occasion and, like many good restaurants, even provided coats and ties at the door for all who needed them.

But here was a man walking around the party unshaven and in his grubbies. So God asked him what he was doing there without a coat and tie. The man was speechless, for it was obvious he had forced his way in refusing to abide by the dress code.

Well, God is gracious, but he hates to be presumed upon. Here was a man as insolent and arrogant and ungrateful as his former wholesalers, distributors, and retailers. God had had enough of that, so there was only one thing to do with this brazen party-crasher — throw him out. And that's precisely what the bouncers did.

And that's the way it has been ever since — God lets out his franchises to all who want to be involved in his business. And they can keep the franchise so long as they remember whose business it is and abide by his rules.

And lover of a good time that he is, God still has big, happy, scrumptious dinner parties. And he invites everyone. But if anyone starts to presume upon God by refusing to abide by the dress code, he is disinvited real fast.

So God's great invitation keeps going out again and again all over the world. Everyone is invited, but not everyone chooses to accept. Strange, isn't it? What are you going to do about your invitation?

Prayer

Eternal God, by whose power and love the buds of spring burst their enclosures to blossom into radiant beauty, and by whose design the birds of the forest sing their thousands of different songs for the enrichment of life; we come to you as your grateful people who are able to share in the ecstasy of the world. In every particle of nature there is the faithful and complex work of millions of cells making a leaf here, a flower there, a brain somewhere else. Who can comprehend it all and take it in? It is too wonderful for articulation.

But, O Lord God, we come to you not only in ecstasy, but in agony. We think of the agonies of starvation and disease, the agonies of pain and suffering, disappointment and failure. We have the agony of broken dreams and crushed hopes; love lost and labor dissipated. We think too of the agony of man arrayed against man in war and violent conflict; men making discord where harmony was intended, havoc where peace should prevail.

We pray for the inspiration of your Spirit and the guidance of your wisdom that cooperatively we might transform our agony to ecstasy. We confess very often our conceit gets in the way, our distorted sense of self-sufficiency. An exaggerated appraisal of our powers sometimes leads us away from you, O Lord. Our pride leads to arrogance, our arrogance to resentment, our resentment to hostility, our hostility to destruction. Forgive this descending spiral of waywardness, O God, and bring us to yourself with a renewed sense of your purpose and love. Through Jesus Christ our Lord. Amen.

11. The Hunger Pangs Of Success

Have this mind among yourselves, which is yours in Christ Jesus, who, though he was in the form of God, did not count equality with God a thing to be grasped, but emptied himself, taking the form of a servant, being born in the likeness of men. — Philippians 2:5-7

In the 1990s we lived in highly successful times. We had the longest sustained bull market in history, awaiting the huge correction predicted by weary bears and market realists. Month after month, millions of dollars poured into mutual funds and stock portfolios as baby-boomers, who had never experienced a serious market correction or economic recession, stored up more and more for retirement. Even the economically troubled Asian economies failed to arrest the powerful surge toward more and more American wealth and success.

New York City was Boomtown USA largely because of the burgeoning financial markets. Office buildings partially vacant after the '87 crash were filled at premium prices, with new ones going up. Apartment rentals were astronomical, once again putting the squeeze on the middle class to make Manhattan the domain of the very rich or the very poor. The building boom continued and where it will stop, nobody knows.

And the theatres and restaurants love it — especially the restaurants. The *New York Times* reported unprecedented business in the city's finest and most expensive eateries. As year-end bonus money made its way into the bank accounts of Wall Street types, the spending was lavish. The very best of foods was enjoyed in great quantities. And the wines? Well, it was not the medium-priced wines that sold, but the most expensive! Wines at $300, $400, $500 a bottle made their way to the banqueting tables of the very successful in such great quantities, wine stewards had to search the world for additional supplies.

And after the great feasts of obvious opulence and lasting luxury, there were the cigars and port. And not just any cigars and port, but the very best, the most aged and expensive money could buy. It was the scene of wealth, prosperity, and success at its very best. Tom Wolfe's "masters of the universe," described in *Bonfires of the Vanities*, were at it again. They had it all. They were the masters of success. There did not seem to be many pangs of hunger in this crowd.

I.

But the crowd in Jesus' day was a different matter.

It is true the Romans were having their equivalent of a bull market. They were indeed "masters of the universe." They had established their imperial boundaries south to Egypt, East to Persia, North to Pontus, and West to Gaul and Britain. Their powerful, well-trained armies made safe the impressive network of roads Rome had built. Rome's navies had made the sea lanes relatively free of pirates to ensure prosperous trade. Roman architectural accomplishments of stadiums, aqueducts, palaces, government buildings, and shrines reflected the glory and grandeur that was Rome. Success was everywhere. There were no pangs of hunger at Caesar's table. They were stuffed with success.

But of course, Jesus and his people were a different matter. The priests and landowners were doing all right, of course, since they had learned to accommodate Rome and sustain their fortunes, if not their liberty. A few in the miniscule middle classes held their anger in check as they kept their head above financial and political water.

But the peasants — the wretched peasant poor, the subsisting, suffering ninety percent of the population of Jesus' fellow Jews — these poor, famished peasants were quite a different matter. In their aching bellies the pangs for success throbbed with an intensity born of centuries of suffering. In the distended bellies of their little ones, in the drained countenances of laboring mothers, in the lined faces of work-weary men — the longing for success and victory flowed in a subterranean stream of intense hatred and craving hope.

Add to that the memories — the humiliating memories. For the last couple of centuries prior to the Romans, their own leaders had betrayed them with corruption and oppression. Before that it was the Greeks, the Persians, the Babylonians, and the Assyrians. They were God's people after all, or so they had been told. When would they have their day in the sun? When would theirs be the kingdom and the power and the glory? Their whole body politic longed for victory, prayed for vindication, and craved success. Who could blame them if within their deepest self there raged a ferocity of desire, and if within their heart of hearts, a fanatic craving for victory awaited liberation?

So when, nearly 2,000 years ago at Passover, Jesus scanned the gleaming white limestone of Jerusalem in the midday sun, he looked longingly at the city he wished to win for God and his people. And the writhing, aching, malnourished bodies of Jewish peasants looked longingly with him.

As *he* surveyed the thousands of pilgrims there for the High Holy Days, *they* surveyed him as the possible long-awaited Messiah, the prayed-for, hoped-for Davidic liberator. The powerless peasants by the thousands, the beleaguered middle-classes, the secretly hopeful rich — all felt the writhing, pulsating pangs for success in their inner beings.

So the throngs began their long-suppressed shouts to acclaim him King. The muted hopes of the centuries began to find their voice and join the chorus. Palm branches were taken from the trees for a flag fanfare. Cloaks were thrown on the ground as a "red carpet" for the approaching royal King. And the voices gathered in massive chorus to shout as he approached the Holy City:

> *Open to me the gates of*
> *righteousness, that I may*
> *enter through them and give*
> *thanks to the Lord.*
> Amen. Amen.
>
> *This is the gate of the Lord; the*
> *righteous shall enter through it.*
> Amen! Amen!

> *Save us, we beseech thee, O Lord!*
> >   *O Lord, we beseech thee,*
> >   *give us success!*
> *Amen! Amen!*
>
> *Blessed is he who enters in the name*
> >   *of the Lord!*
> *We bless you from the house of the Lord.*
> *The Lord is God, and he has given*
> >   *us light.*
> *Bind the festal procession with branches,*
> >   *up to the horns of the altar!*
>
> *Hosanna! Blessed is he who comes*
> >   *in the name of the Lord*
> *Hosanna! Son of David!*
> *Amen! Amen!*

II.

Centuries later in Amherst, Massachusetts, a sensitive, reclusive literary genius would be perceiving what Jesus was perceiving that day amid the potential power and glory.

> *Success is counted sweetest*
> *By those who ne'er succeed.*
> *To comprehend a nectar*
> *Requires the sorest need.*
> > ("Success Is Counted Sweetest," *The Complete Poems of Emily Dickinson*, ed. Thomas H. Johnson, p. 35)

Feeling the same deep, God-given truth flow through her as flowed through Jesus, Emily Dickinson continued:

> *Not one of all the purple Host*
> *Who took the Flag today*
> *Can tell the definition*
> *So clear of Victory.*

> *As he defeated — dying —*
> *On whose forbidden ear*
> *The distant strains of triumph*
> *Burst agonized and clear!*
> > (*op. cit.*, p. 35)

The disciples, of course, were in their glory in the triumphal parade. Three long, hard years of campaigning up and down dusty Palestine seemed now to be paying off. Three long years of giving up the comforts and securities of home and family. Three long years of giving up income, living on campaign contributions, while their competitors went on to build up their fortunes (meager as they were). Three long years of a different town, a different bed, and different food on the rubber chicken circuit every night. Three long years of success and accolade, counter-balanced with ridicule and rejection. Three long years coming at last to cherished victory and overwhelming success.

Yes, open for us the gates of righteousness that we might take this city and nation by storm and make at last this country our own. This is the day the Lord has made. We are rejoicing at last in the promised victory. Save us now! Grant us victory! Give us success! On to victory. We will be the "masters of the universe."

> *Much madness is divinest Sense —*
> *To a discerning Eye —*
> *Much sense — the starkest Madness —*
> *'Tis the majority*
> *In This, as All, prevail —*
> *Assent — and you are sane —*
> *Demur — you're straightway dangerous —*
> *And handled with a Chain —*
> > ("Much Madness Is Divinest Sense," Emily Dickinson *op. cit.*, p. 209)

Yes, with a chain and a cross too! In that subterranean stream of divinest sense tapped by poets and prophets, Emily Dickinson saw what Jesus saw and knew in his heart of hearts. He saw, he knew, the majority of the shouting thousands in the crowd were wrong.

He saw it and he knew it as he rode down the steep side of the Mount of Olives, on past the Garden of Gethsemane, across the Brook Kidron, on up the slope to the Eastern gate of the Temple Mount area wherein the Messiah was to appear. He saw it and knew it as he looked into the eyes of the cheering thousands — the eyes filled not only with longing, but with revenge; eyes filled not only with hope, but with the age-old lust to get even. He could feel it in the voices grown hoarse and coarse with shouting — the bloodthirsty, blood-curdling cries for holy war, for *herem*, for holocaust. Obliterate the enemy, kill every man, woman, and child. Let the enemy's blood flow in our rivers to the sea.

In their own way, in their own bloodless way, Tom Wolfe's "masters of the universe" in his *Bonfires of the Vanities* did just that. Sitting as they did at the junction of rivers of massive fortunes ebbing and flowing, turning and twisting at their control, they had it all. It was all theirs — money, power, women, prestige, influence, prosperity, security, almost immortality itself. Except in Sherman McCoy it all came apart, came tumbling down, dissipated in affairs and confrontations, in mistakes and reversals, collapsing in the weight of opulence without conscience, and colliding with reality in the blindness of pride and arrogance.

Yes, it is true Jesus seemed to make a move to be "master of the universe." Yes, it is true, he did throw out the moneychangers who represented the multimillion-dollar business of selling animals for sacrifice and changing foreign currency into Temple shekels. Yes, it is true his disciples were there by the thousands, many of them armed, no doubt, to lead an uprising and coup much like Judas Maccabaeus and his brothers a couple of centuries earlier.

But instead of taking the city by storm, he wept over it. Instead of seizing the moment and taking the tide at its full, he lost his fortunes. Instead of fulfilling the promise to feed the stomachs of the thousands of peasant poor with bread, he was haunted by the deeper truth that man does not live by bread alone. Instead of seizing power and glory for himself and his people, he seemed to throw it aside to his enemies. Instead of coming into the glory and power and fullness of his Kingdom, he rides on to an ignoble and humiliating death of utter weakness and despicable mockery.

O Jerusalem, thou that killest the prophets, would that even now, you the city, whose name means, "vision of peace" — would that even now you knew the things that make for peace, but they are hidden from your eyes, so lamented Jesus.

It's a terrible truth, one we choke on and gag on every year at this time — the truth that he who exalts himself will be humbled; the truth that he who is first will be last, and the last first; the truth that the first in the Kingdom of God is the one who serves rather than the one who domineers; the truth that those who seek to save their life will lose it, but those who lose their life for the sake of God will find it; the truth — the strange truth — that the hunger pangs of success are quieted in self-denial rather than self-exaltation. For what shall it profit a person if he or she gains the whole world and loses his or her very soul, his or her very self?

It is that strange, strange, set of truths Jesus saw that tumultuous, triumphant day in Jerusalem. Jerusalem and Judea indeed, the whole world itself, cannot satisfy the hunger pangs for the soul's success. Man's achievement never can do it. It is God's gift. It is God's gift of grace through faith.

So he came into the city in glory amid the waving palms and shouting thousands on a "red robe carpet" of threadbare peasant cloaks, thrown jubilantly, expectantly from suffering peasants famished for success. Into the city with shouts of Hosanna. And out of the city to the shouts of crucify, crucify. Into the city amid waving palm branches. Out of the city flogged with the cat of nine tails. Into the city with proffers of victory banquets and rarest of wines; out of the city to derisive spit and vile cursing. Into the city on the beast of the peaceful King; out of the city on the cross of the condemned criminal.

O Jesus, Jesus. Jesus didn't you get it wrong? Didn't you miss the flood tide when it came? Didn't you miss your chance for fame and glory? Didn't you fail in your bid for your place in the eternal sun?

No, says the great apostle, Paul. He did not try to gain immortality by violence. Instead, he humbled himself and became obedient unto death, so now God had highly exalted him so that all who believe in him might have *eternal* life and the deep, deep satisfaction of food for our famished souls.

> *Why do you spend your money for*
> *that which is not bread,*
> *and your labor for that*
> *which does not satisfy?*

So asked the prophet Isaiah long ago.

> *Incline you ear, and come to me;*
> *hear, that your soul may live ...*
> *says the Lord.* — 55:2-3

And paradox of paradox, irony of ironies, the exalted Jesus now says to all one and one-half billion of his followers all over the world, "I am the bread of life; he who comes to me shall not hunger, and he who believes in me shall not thirst ... I am the living bread which came down from heaven; if any one eats of this bread he will live forever ..." (John 6:35, 51). And satisfy the hunger pangs of success.

Prayer

O Eternal God, whose power sustains the universe and whose vital Spirit pulsates in all living things, we praise you for all the splendor of spring and for all the glory of life bursting forth from winter rest. Even now as our northern earth tilts itself toward your life-giving sun, even so would we tilt ourselves, with any winter coldness of heart, toward you, our Eternal Sun. We praise and adore you, O God, and in this sacred time and place seek your holy presence.

On this holy day when we celebrate Jesus' triumphal entry into Jerusalem, we think of our own longings for victory and triumph in our own lives. In business or profession, in family or career, we seek the satisfactions not only of success, but the rewards of the inner contentment of the soul. Help us always to direct our lives in ways that will be both honorable and fulfilling.

And for those of us who have failed, for those of us who have had reverses and setbacks, for those of us discouraged and suffering from depression — for those of us defeated now, bring a new sense of hope and a new resolve to move forward in the pilgrimage you have planned for us.

We pray for those with special needs — for those doing battle with disease, for those in fractured relationships, for those alienated and estranged, for those mourning loved ones. Grant them your strength and blessing according to their need. Through Jesus Christ our Lord. Amen.

12. Dinner At Emmaus

When he was at table with them, he took the bread and blessed it, and broke it, and gave it to them. And their eyes were opened and they recognized him ... Then they told how he was known to them in the breaking of the bread.
— Luke 24:30-31, 35

*It is a beauteous evening, calm and free
The holy time is quiet as a nun
Breathless with adoration; the broad sun
Is sinking down in its tranquility;
The gentleness of heaven broods o'er the sea;
Listen. God being with (us) when we know it not.*

As William Wordsworth described an evening walk with his wife and child, so might he have described a Sunday evening walk of centuries ago from Jerusalem to the village of Emmaus. Two followers of Jesus were returning home from the Passover festivities in the Holy City.

Although they had been shaken by the events of the betrayal, the illegal trial, and the humiliating crucifixion, there was a feeling in the air on their way home, the sense of calm following a tragedy, a feeling that enabled them to say with Wordsworth,

*It is a beauteous evening, calm and free,
The holy time is quiet as a nun
Breathless with adoration....*

We imagine that first Easter evening to be one of glorious but gentle sunset, with rays of light orchid, orange, and red filtering through the fine mist above the Mediterranean with the hint of Palestinian dust in the air. It was an evening of extraordinary tranquility — of strange peace — an inexplicable peace following an upheaval of history and the defeat of cherished visions and dreams.

The two disciples — Cleopas and Simon — were discussing the awesome events of the past week when they were joined by a stranger. They were surprised he did not seem to know what had happened. But their feelings were intense and they readily expressed their dismay. "We had hoped," they said, "that Jesus of Nazareth would deliver Israel from her enemies and establish her in power again, as in the time of David. But the chief priests and rulers crucified him and once again we are without hope."

The stranger reviewed some of the Messianic prophecies with them and pointed out how the scriptures suggested the Messiah would suffer before entering his glory. The discussion continued as they drew near to the village of Emmaus, so Cleopas and Simon, extending customary Near Eastern hospitality, asked the stranger to stay with them for the night.

When they reclined at table for dinner, the soft, orchid glow of the Mediterranean sky and the subtle radiance of the oil lamps cast a mysterious, eternal patina over the scene worthy of a Rembrandt. In a strange switch of roles, the stranger acted as host instead of guest. He took the bread, blessed it, broke it, and gave it to them. Suddenly, they recognized the Easter evening stranger as the risen Jesus.

In the midst of their throbbing excitement, he vanished from them, and they said to one another, "Did not our hearts burn within us while he talked to us on the road, while he opened to us the scriptures?" Immediately they rushed back to Jerusalem and told the eleven apostles how he had made himself known to them in the breaking of bread at dinner in Emmaus. It was at dinner in Emmaus, these two disciples had their lives radically altered. If we come in spirit and imagination to Emmaus, we also can be changed. The presence of the living God can be made more real to us.

I.

In Eastertide, we are reminded by the dinner at Emmaus that God can be made known to us through the *Sacred Scriptures*.

After they had recognized the stranger as the Risen Christ, the disciples remembered, "Did not our hearts burn within us while he talked to us on the road, while he opened to us the scriptures?" The phrase, "hearts burn within us," suggests a vivid sense of presence, a hint of being on the brink of discovery, an awareness of a new reality breaking in. It suggests the "Aha" experience of which philosophers speak, or the "Oh, I see" exclamation of one who has just found a key to a puzzling mystery.

Notice that in the Emmaus experience Jesus does not quote abstract philosophy or abstruse poetry. He does not recite an awe-inspiring soliloquy, nor does he engage in complex and confusing sophistry. Instead, he calls their attention to scriptures they already know, to passages and concepts already familiar, to ways of imaging the world and reality that already have been experienced. But as the great master teacher he was, he enabled them to see the sacred realities in a new light — so much so that the presence of the living God came to them afresh.

Very often the sense of the presence of God is absent from us because we do not know the Sacred Scriptures. While the Bible is the world's most-sold book, it often remains the least-read book. It, along with Shakespeare, is respected but seldom dusted by regular use. Consequently, we suffer not only from appalling biblical illiteracy, but also from a gnawing sense of the absence of God.

Barbara Walters recently had a special program on television discussing why American children flunk. There were many reasons cited, but a recurring one was absence of parental concern and discipline. American parents seemed to be preoccupied with making money and maintaining a high standard of living, even at the expense of poorly educated children. Many European and Asian educational systems far surpass our own, making us wonder about America's future leadership role.

Barbara Walters might do another special on biblical and religious literacy. One mature Christian gentleman thought Moses and Jesus were more or less contemporary, while in fact, Moses preceded Jesus by about thirteen centuries. Many church people cannot name the four Gospels. Very few can name the books of the Bible and most are confused as to which books belong in the Old or New Testaments. If we were to ask, "Does the book of Hezekiah belong in the Old or New Testament?" how would you answer? I hope you responded, "Neither," because there is no such biblical book.

Of course, such questions deal only with superficial knowledge. We are more concerned with the essential message of the Bible, its central truths and main teachings. Over and over again it is the Church's testimony that the Sacred Scriptures have the power to make real the presence of God in our own time.

In some ways it should come as no surprise that conservative and fundamentalist churches are growing. While their narrowness and rigidity and dogmatism would be unacceptable to many of us, they do, nevertheless, bear witness to the great biblical truths over against the secular whims and ephemeral vagaries of the present age.

The biblical witness is perhaps even more powerful in China, South Korea, Indonesia, and other Pacific Rim countries where Christianity is growing like wildfire. It is predicted South Korea soon will be over fifty percent Christian. Some say China will be Christian by the mid-twenty-first century. Over against other mythologies and philosophies, the Sacred Scriptures demonstrate the power to manifest the presence of the living Christ.

Therefore, is it not time for our so-called liberal mainline churches to abandon pseudo-sophistication and religious dalliance to get up to date on biblical knowledge? Is it not time to make an assault on our appalling biblical illiteracy at all age levels? If some of us have argued for a return to basics in our general educational system so that high school graduates can at least write a grammatically correct sentence — if we have argued for a return to basics there, why not also in religion?

We can be sure the world is going to live by some religion or philosophy or mythology. Islam is growing rapidly, as is Buddhism. If Christians are going to lead the world, they are going to have to be educated in the basics.

Along the road to Emmaus, the risen Jesus quoted the scriptures to expound to them the will and wisdom of God, so much so their hearts burned within them. The late J. B. Phillips, well-known British translator of the New Testament, wrote of his experience as he translated from Greek to English. He said as he was working on the Gospels, a living person emerged out of the words, the living person of Jesus Christ. That sometimes has been our experience. Have not our hearts burned within us as we have opened the scriptures together?

II.

The presence of the risen, living Christ was also made known to them in the *breaking of bread*.

Food plays a large part in most religions. Bread and wine are, of course, central to the Christian sacrament as they have been central to other religions. Most religions have festivals or feast days. Even the gods are thought by some to eat and drink the sacrifices offered to them. Food and drink are the very source of life. Nature feeds on itself — protein eating protein. And nature in turn feeds on the sun — on light — for photosynthesis, the basic manufacturing process of the living cells of all plants. Thus, in a real sense we live off light. Food is encapsulated light. Therefore, it is no wonder religion would deal with something so basic as food — the source of life, which comes from light, or energy.

Ironically, religious people cannot quite decide if feasting or fasting makes them more religious. John the Baptist shunned civilization, lived in the wilderness in rude clothing, fasting on locusts and wild honey. Some people thought he was very religious, but others said he was a wild man, that he had a demon.

Jesus, on the other hand, came eating and drinking. He attended wedding feasts and banquets. He frequently was invited to dinner parties with the outsiders as well as the insiders, much to the chagrin of the insiders. Many thought Jesus was religious, though critics accused him of being a glutton and drunkard because he was at so many feasts and parties. Jesus did practice fasting and he recommended it. But he also enjoyed feasting, breaking bread, and sharing wine.

I confess I have much preferred the religion of Jesus over that of John the Baptist; the joy and conviviality of wedding feasts and dinner parties over the austerity and loneliness of the wilderness with its locusts and wild honey. This preference apparently goes back to my early childhood. My wife and children delight in telling about my first grade report card they found in the attic and the grades I received. They point out with delight that I received an "A" for lunch.

So it is, when Jesus reclined at table in Emmaus, he blessed the bread and broke it in such a familiar fashion that there was a rush of recognition, a vivid sense of familiarity. In the common act of breaking and sharing the bread of life, the divine presence was experienced. Although it was a common meal at Emmaus, it became uncommonly sacramental. The uncommon became known in the commonplace.

Therefore, the Church rightly has placed bread-breaking at the center of its worship. It is in the homely and familiar that the divine is known. It is not necessary to strive after unearthly ecstasies, drug-induced or not. We are not dealing with abstruse formulas, secret incantations, mysterious passwords, philosophical abstractions, or sophist relativities where my theory is as good as yours.

We are not dealing with unusual or abnormal rites like sacrificing a virgin to make the sun rise or sacrificing humans as done recently by a cult in Mexico. Nor are we asked to kiss cobras or handle rattlesnakes or sacrifice an animal or climb Mount Everest. Instead, we are assured the living Christ wishes to make himself known in the common, everyday act of breaking bread, an act available to the most common among us.

However, the idea of breaking bread as spiritual act has been neglected in our frenetic, fast-paced times. If breaking bread once was associated with leisure, with sustenance both physical and spiritual, and with getting to know others, today breaking bread is often done on the run or at the desk or in the car. It recently was reported that some of America's richest men do not enjoy good food. They only eat to work to make more money. Consequently, for many, breaking bread is only a necessary evil to make us more productive.

Oh, to be sure, we enjoy our culinary delights. As Tom Wolfe says, we all strive to be seen in the latest "restaurant of the century" where the owner-chef serves as a kind of high priest of the in-group, of those truly initiated into the mysteries of status and the state of "having arrived." It is salvation through sophisticated salivation. We are "in" because the "in" foods are in us.

Contrast these stressful, prideful, anxiety-ridden dinners with the revelation and self-revelation that occurred at Emmaus and other dinner parties. Jesus often used the occasion of sharing physical food as the vehicle for spiritual nourishment. Not only did people come to understand God and Jesus while at table; they came to understand *themselves*.

But few of us take the time or leisure to know or be known. In a recent *Christian Science Monitor* column, Marilyn Gardner describes ours as the "Workaholic Generation" of the "high-performance life." Quoting *Fortune* magazine she notes that the Baby Boomers put in grueling hours, from sixty to ninety hours a week (April 11, 1989, p. 14).

The cover headline sums up: "Their energy is high, their hours hellish, and their reward is — what?" Ms. Gardner then suggests a certain leisure to "construct the true fabric of the self." In place of the rushing, pushing, striving, stretching thin, let there be a leisurely meal where we speak and listen and share the wine, and know, and are known in breaking bread.

III.

However, at the dinner in Emmaus, the presence of the living Christ was also made known through the reality of the *transformed body*. Luke says "their eyes were opened and they recognized him."

People in every age struggle with cranial arthritis and spiritual rheumatism. Narrowness of mind and smallness of spirit are not limited to religious people. Politicians and businessmen suffer from them as do housewives and teachers. Doctors and lawyers often become stagnant, as do social workers and economists. Old, familiar, but worn-out ideas cling to us as stubbornly as barnacles to boat bottoms. But the experience of the disciples at Emmaus literally blew their minds. It was beyond their dreams and expectations, and that makes it so authentic. They experienced the objective reality of the risen Christ which released them from a dead past to an exciting, living future.

Many of us are disciples of the past rather than participants in the present and future. We have done a "freeze-frame" of some past "peak experience" or understanding of reality and have made it normative forever.

Consider how radically changed is the world of science. We used to say matter can neither be created nor destroyed. But that scientific dogma was literally blown apart at Hiroshima. Whereas once many were dogmatic materialists, we now affirm with author Barry Wood that "matter is patterning energy and energy is radiating matter" (*The Magnificent Frolic*, p. 160).

Or consider the recently announced breakthrough in nuclear fusion — not fission, but fusion. In an amazingly simple experiment two American scientists seem to have produced nuclear fusion from simple seawater. Harnessing the same energy process used by the sun, this breakthrough may absolutely revolutionize our energy sources. Our doubt and skepticism about new realities says far more about us than it does about the wonders of the universe.

Doubters and skeptics tend to be too much people of the past. The man of the past, says British theologian H. A. Williams, "trusts in his accumulated mental constructs and mistakes them for reality." Added to that, says Williams, may be a "spiritual sloth," "an unwillingness to allow reality to impinge upon us because of all the trouble it will cause. We may be too lazy to take our bearings afresh. We do not want to reorient ourselves. We may not want ... to repent. It is easier to continue working vigorously in the old rut ..." (*True Resurrection*, p. 94).

The disciples at Emmaus had to revise radically all their old religious concepts and dogmatisms. The careful formulas and accepted norms regarding God had to be revised upward. God, they discovered, was not in their box or Joseph's tomb. God was alive and well and leading into the future. Unlike many religious types always wanting to call us *back* to God, as if he were entrapped in some nostalgic past, the Risen Christ is always calling us *forward* to God. In God's eyes, the world and the Church are forever "behind the times." The arrogance of secularism is that this age is "it," that this time is "the" time, and our people "the" people. But such stopping the clock to freeze-frame our constructs will never do. God is on the move. God is process.

One writer lamenting the demise of the American railroads said the first step to revitalizing the railroads was to throw out all the old railroad people with outdated ideas and habits. Corporations losing business often first have to change within as Ross Perot thought General Motors needed to do.

Mainline churches are like the corporations who have lost their corner of the business and thus conclude there is no market. But the market is there. Forty-four percent of Americans are unchurched. Mainline churches are now sideline churches because they live too much in the past. The market has changed and moved away from them.

If the world is no longer buying Edsels, then the Church ought to stop making them. We are not being called *back* to God, but *forward* to God. We need to stop being a sideline Church and become a frontline Church.

At the dinner in Emmaus centuries ago, the living Christ became real to the disciples through scripture, the breaking of bread and the transformed body which necessitated a transformed way of seeing. He came to them unexpectedly, surprisingly, unusually, and they had the courage to receive him, to change, to be born anew to the new realities. In personal communion with him, their own identity became clearer and the magnificence of God's new reality was glimpsed. As we go to dinner at Emmaus in imagination, may the same happen to us.

Prayer

Eternal God, who with springtime rains makes the world lush and green, and who with the tilt of the earth toward the light, draws forth buds and blossoms to radiate beauty to all eyes of beholders, praise be to you for the delicate majesty of your handiwork. We thank you for faithfully blessing us with light and life temporal and everlasting.

If flock and field live by your water and light and thus sustain our bodies, even more do all things come to be from you, uncreated light of light. When our bodies have had their fill of bread and wine, our minds and souls hunger still for the living bread, and thirst after the living water from which drinking we shall never thirst again.

Break now the bread of life to us, O Lord. Help us to taste and see how gracious you are compared to all the legalisms and vanities of man we ingest as daily bread for the mind. If in the anxiety of living we have chased one fleeting idea after another, help us to focus firmly on you, central idea of all that is. If in the risks of dreadful freedom we have clutched mental menus and residual recipes now moldy and stale, give us courage to move forward to your new culinary delights. If in our exodus from the bondage to the past we long for the leeks and onions and flesh pots of Egypt, help us to receive your heavenly manna with gratefulness and to look forward to the milk and honey of your promised land.

O God of the future, who calls us to be a pilgrim people following you, the cloud by day, the pillar of fire by night, feasting on your word of truth, so fill us now with your light and life that we might be radiant, exuberant, full of joy for the victories of the future that are to be ours. In Christ's name we pray. Amen.

13. Breakfast On The Beach

When they came ashore, they saw a charcoal fire there, with fish laid on it, and some bread ... Jesus said, Come and have breakfast.
— John 21:9, 12 (NEB)

It is early morning on the lake. The solemn quiet is interrupted only by the gentle surf upon the sand. In the distance a bird is announcing the dawn with his centuries-old song. Soft light trickles through the subtle mist. From the dew the white sand is slightly moist, and we sit entranced in the stillness, the beauty, the peace.

Our reverie is broken by voices across the water, somewhat gruff and weary. Gradually the outline of a boat appears, and we see the wet fishnet glisten slightly in the emerging light and hear the net weights splash the water uniformly, thrown by experienced fishermen hands. Coming closer the boat reveals seven men, grousing and grumbling, throwing their nets mechanically, half-heartedly, expecting little, getting nothing.

Clearing our eyes we look down the beach and notice in the early morning chill, smoke rising easily from an inviting fire. Intermittently, the faint aroma of food cooking reaches us, and we are tempted to join the stranger around the fire.

About that time the stranger shouts to the fishermen, "Friends, have you caught anything?" He asked the question in a tone that suggested he already knew what we knew. The fishermen replied as we expected. The stranger then shouted, "Throw your net to the right side of the boat and try your luck there." Perhaps from his vantagepoint he could see a shoal of fish. There was a moment of hesitation on the boat, but then they reasoned, why not. What could they lose?

With the net heavy and full, the disappointed, sullen fishermen awakened to the excitement of success. And in the awakening they took a more careful look at the stranger in the early morning light. "It is the Lord," exclaimed John. A shock went through the whole group. From the beach we could see the electric awareness. Then one of the men, clad only in his loincloth, threw on a kind of shirt, jumped into the water and swam ashore to greet the stranger. The others remained in the boat, struggling to bring in the huge catch of fish.

About then the stranger called out, "Come have breakfast. And bring some of the fish you have caught." (They had caught 153.) We can see the charcoal fire is just right now for broiling fresh fish and toasting bread. Soon the hungry fishermen are embracing the stranger, warming themselves by the fire, and talking quietly among themselves, though excitedly. And just now we feel our hunger pangs and wish we could join in the warmth of that fire and the excited camaraderie of the group there with the unique stranger. Let's draw a little closer.

I.

Now we are beginning to see more clearly. These men are some of the disciples. There are Peter, James, and John, Thomas the twin, Nathaniel, and two others. And the stranger is Jesus — the Risen Christ.

We know the story well. After the crucifixion, the disciples had locked themselves behind closed doors in Jerusalem, for fear they too would be executed as traitors. Eventually, at least those seven escaped to the north, to Galilee, to their homes and families and former businesses.

It was difficult to do. They fully expected the ridicule and mockery of their wiser friends and family members who had decided to stay home rather than follow Jesus. Their worst fears had been confirmed. Jesus had been killed like all the other would-be Messiahs. So now, defeated and humiliated, they had come home to take up their old work.

So Peter, James, and John invited the others to go fishing with them. It was great to be back. Peter loved the smell of the sea. It always was a thrill to hoist the simple sail and to feel the wind move his boat out into the deeper water. The lines and nets were familiar in his hands. From long experience he knew all the landmarks along the shore. There's that special clump of trees. And over there is that peculiar house. And there is that unusual rock.

Ah, the old familiar places, how they helped to ease the pain of failure. In many ways it was great to be back home, doing the things he had been taught from his youth. Maybe this was where he really belonged. Maybe he was a fool to have dreamed his dreams of deliverance and liberation. Visionaries always do get you in trouble, he thought, as he pulled on the tiller. Once you break out of your accustomed role that has been given you, you can easily be fooled. But no one could fool him about fishing. He had learned that from childhood and could hold his own with the best. And so he fell back into his old way of life, trying to forget his dreams of a new future, with a new Messiah and a new Kingdom, and an exciting new day in history.

We have felt the same. Have there not been times when this Jesus excited us, when he aroused our hopes, enlarged our vision, and breathed fresh vigor into these weary lives? Have we not enjoyed, from time to time, the fresh burst of hope, the resurgence of faith, and the longing to believe again in the reality of love? Maybe it came on Easter amidst the trumpets and bells and the grand hallelujah of Christ's resurrection.

But then on Monday, life settles into its dull routine. You argue with your husband. The business is plagued with problems. There is friction in personal relationships. So we forget about Easter, and fall back into the old ways, allowing ourselves to be engulfed by the habitual depressing attitudes.

We had heard the call to adventure, but then in disappointment and fear, settled back into the old ways of defeat and death. Antoine de Saint-Exupery describes us well when he claims we lock ourselves up in our own prisons of fear and despair, opting for comfort and security rather than adventure. He says,

> *You rolled yourself up into a ball in your genteel security, in routine, in the stifling conversations of provincial life, raising a modest rampart against the winds and the tides and the stars. You have chosen not to be*

> *perturbed by great problems, having trouble enough to forget your own fate as man ... Nobody grasped you by the shoulder while there was still time. Now the clay of which you were shaped has dried and hardened, and naught in you will awaken the sleeping musician, the poet, the astronomer that possibly inhabited you in the beginning.* (Wind, Sand and Stars, p. 11)

Is there still time to rescue you, to awaken the potential within you? Had you been stirred to a resurrection of hope and new relationships, only to be discouraged, and to say forget it, and to return to business as usual as did Peter and the disciples?

But now this Risen Christ calls to us from the warmth of his charcoal fire and he says, "Come join us for breakfast. Here, have some crisp, broiled fish and some warm, toasted bread." And he assures us we were not fools after all, that his cause will not end in humiliation and defeat, that love and newness of life will triumph. And so we feel the old excitement return and our hearts warm up again and the smile returns. And have you noticed how much more beautiful the world looks?

II.

Now that we've been drawn into the circle around the charcoal fire, let's sit down a while. The sand is warm and dry now, and look, the sun is coming up. It's burning off the mist. Notice the deep blue of the sky and the reflection in the lake. Now the horizon is clearing. Just the beauty alone is enough to renew our vigor. But sitting around the fire with the mysterious sense of Christ's presence is more invigorating still. And without question, those early disciples were confident of his presence and power, so much so, they changed the world.

But now, of course, the years have come and gone. Human life has had its share of suffering and tragedy. Then too, it has had its successes, and some of us have become satiated with good things, and yet we are flaccid and often bored. So we long again for an invigorating sense of Christ's presence. How do we get it?

One way is that of following the principle of great musicians. Claudio Arrau, the great concert pianist, underwent many years of psychoanalysis before he came to his superior level of artistry. He had great difficulty for some time. His playing lacked the life and sparkle and depth of feeling he knew it should have.

Eventually, said Arrau, I learned the secret of truly great artistry. I learned that I, the artist, must decrease, and the music and the composer must increase. I had always put myself at the center, said Arrau, and I got nowhere. But then I was determined to put the music and mind of the composer at center. So now, in each concert I reach and reach for the soul and mind of Brahms or Beethoven, and I am released from my own ego to express the fullness of their music. It is then Brahms and Beethoven came alive to the audience. They, in a way, sense their presence, as do I.

We do not, as Christians, have a musical score to follow. But we do have a Bible and the traditions and hymns of the church. And our experience is that when we place our own egos aside and reach for the mind and soul of Christ, he comes alive to us and to the group in a unique way as a living presence. It is as though we can feel him here and detect his firm power and gentle wisdom shaping the nature of our gathering.

III.

Listen as the conversation continues around the fire. The sun is higher now. The outline of the hills is more distinct. We see other fishing boats making their way back to the docks and the morning market. We've nearly finished this delicious charbroiled fish and bread. And we sense something important coming up.

Jesus now turns to Peter, asking him if he loves him. Peter assures him he does. But Jesus doesn't seem satisfied and again he raises the question. Peter answers affirmatively. A third time Jesus puts the question, "Simon, Son of John, do you love me?" Peter, nearly exasperated, says "Lord, you know all things, you know I love you."

Notice Jesus didn't call him Peter, which means rock. Rather, he addresses him by his old name of Simon, son of John, because that's what he was now that he had forsaken Christ and returned to his fishing and his old way of life. And because of Peter's earlier three-time denial, he hardly could be solid as a rock. So he pressed the question of love three times to offset the three-time denial. But once the new allegiance was sworn, Jesus urged him to take leadership again in feeding the sheep, in watching over the Christian flock.

So it was at breakfast on the beach Peter was reminded of the importance of the human relationships they had begun as a part of the Kingdom of God. Their ties of everlasting friendship were renewed, ties that were more important than fishing or boats or profits.

Antoine de St. Exupery observes:

> *We forget that there is no hope of joy except in human relations. If I summon up those memories that have left me an enduring savor, if I draw up the balance sheet of the hours in my life that have truly counted, surely I find only those that no wealth could have procured me. True riches cannot be bought. One cannot buy the friendship of ... a companion to whom one is bound forever by ordeals suffered in common.* (ibid., p. 26)

Antoine continues, "Happiness! It is useless to seek it elsewhere than in this warmth of human relations. Our sordid interests imprison us within their walls. Only a comrade can grasp us by the hand and haul us free" (*ibid.*). That is what Jesus is doing with Peter and the others — breaking down the prison walls of their despair with the assurance of his comradeship. He affirms for them again the unbroken bonds of their relationship, even in the midst of their denials and faithlessness. Once again he entrusts them with the responsibilities of leadership in this movement destined to change the world.

Gathered around the charcoal fire with the last bits of fish consumed we see Jesus' gaze shift to us. We know how often our faith has faded in the high noon realities of life. We've done our share of denying and our returning to the old familiar ways of making money, and of thinking, and of behaving, ways of the old man and the old world.

But now, in the afterglow of Easter, at breakfast on the beach, he asks us if we love him and if we will feed his sheep. For it is in service, in the acts of love and thoughtfulness, in the causes of truth and justice, we begin to sense anew his presence. It is in the acts of following and obedience the knowledge of God becomes more complete and certain. It is the one who keeps the commands of love who is assured more and more of his risen presence.

So now the sun is fully up and the new day has arrived. The charcoal glow has dimmed and Jesus seems ready to be on his way. What a refreshing morning, and how invigorating this breakfast on the beach. Yes, Lord, we do love you. Yes, we will do our part to feed your sheep.

Prayer

Eternal God, who by your creative power has begun to touch the earth in beauty with the first blush of spring; and who, in the afterglow of Easter, has infused a new confidence within our souls that life will win over death, praise be to you for the hope you give us in this season.

We give you thanks for the thrill and exhilaration of new life. We stand amazed at the life forms pulsating, throbbing, beating, manifesting themselves in every living thing in this springtime. We shall ever be amazed at why it is and how it is that the same basic material is organized into a multiplicity of life forms. You astound us day by day with all your marvels, Lord, and we thank you that you have made us participants in your grand experiment of life and love.

In this season of new life and resurrection from the dead, it is for us to confess how easy it is to get back into old ruts and graves. In the dazzling light of new self-knowledge, we often have retreated into old rationalizations and self-justifications. Thrust into new contexts which challenge our old presuppositions, we are slow to learn but quick to defend some outmoded self-concept or self-understanding. Forgive the way we cling to the security of old tombs, and grant us courage to allow you to raise us from the ways of our dead past.

O loving Father of us all, who takes special pity on those who fail, and who is ever ready to seek the lost and to lift up the fallen, look upon us with compassion. We often have declared our love and loyalty for you and our Master, Jesus Christ, only to find ourselves disguising our loyalties when we are beside alien campfires. In our days of hope and idealism we have sworn allegiance to your Cause, only on some dark night to have our loyalties falter and our morals compromised. Be merciful to us, forgive us, and restore us to yourself and grant us the second chance we need. Through Jesus Christ our Lord. Amen.

14. The Ultimate Wedding Reception

And the angel said to me "Write this: Blessed are those who are invited to the marriage supper of the Lamb." — Revelation 19:9

I've been hearing it a lot lately — something most of you have heard as well. I suppose holidays remind us of the truth expressed by many when they say, "About the only time our family ever gets together is for weddings and funerals."

Many would agree, and then reminisce with one lady who recently recalled her youth and childhood and holidays. "We not only got together for weddings and funerals," she said, "we were also together for the major holidays, for birthdays and anniversaries. I really miss that," she continued. "All my aunts and uncles and cousins lived within a few miles of each other. I really miss those happy experiences of my extended family."

I suppose most of us can identify with her. I surely can, for I had a similar childhood with most of my relatives within a reasonable distance. But now, even our own children and their families are scattered from Boston to Minneapolis to San Francisco. And even for us it is often the case that weddings or funerals are the occasions that draw us all together.

But of course, my experience of weddings and funerals extends well beyond family. I have conducted the funerals and stood by the graves of hundreds, saying those familiar words, "Earth to earth, ashes to ashes, and dust to dust," as the earthly farewells were uttered.

And I have married hundreds of couples over the years and attended nearly as many wedding receptions. In recent years, it has been difficult for families to reminisce much at wedding receptions because the band is so loud. And if at table we attempt to converse above the band, they turn up the volume even more. After shouting myself hoarse, I finally resort to smiling benignly at my tablemates, as I worry about subsequent loss of hearing!

Nevertheless, weddings and funerals have much in common. Both have a way of bringing the family together. Both mark beginnings and endings; the ending of singledom and the beginning of martial bliss (or so we hope!). Weddings and funerals suggest sorrow and celebration, the so-called loss of a son or daughter, but on the other hand, the gain of a son or daughter. And funerals involve obvious loss, and then hopefully promise of the gain of life after death. And with both weddings and funerals, there is usually food, a banquet or reception.

In our text we have both a funeral and a wedding. There is the death of Babylon or Rome, the symbol of the old order of oppression and corruption and death. And there is the wedding — the heavenly wedding of God and his people with the ultimate wedding reception.

I.

Let's consider first the funeral.

The other day at lunch at a local restaurant, by chance I sat next to a husband and wife who were acquaintances of mine. On a previous occasion or two we had shared pleasantries. And inasmuch as I was reading some books, he learned I was a minister and adjunct college professor. And I learned he was a retired college professor, now teaching part-time as an adjunct. "You have to keep the mind active," he said, "otherwise it goes dull." His wife nodded in agreement!

Throughout lunch our conversation continued. His wife was very active in her synagogue and adored her rabbi from whom she learned so much. "But," she lamented, "I can't get my husband to share my enthusiasm for our religion." He quickly came to his defense saying, "I don't know, but as I get older, I get more cynical."

I joked with him saying it's supposed to work the other way around. Most people, as they contemplate meeting their Maker face to face, become more vigorous in their faith. That is one reason the Florida churches are packed with octogenarians. When one Florida minister encouraged his people to appreciate God's miracles, one old-timer said, "Young man, every day I wake up is a miracle!"

Ogden Nash wrote about that perspective in his whimsical poem, "Crossing the Border." He says:

> *Senescence begins*
> *And middle age ends*
> *The day your descendents*
> *Outnumber your friends.*
> (*I Wouldn't Have Missed It*, p. 312)

And we have become more and more conscious of that at funerals, where so many we once knew and loved are no longer with us, and our descendents do indeed outnumber our friends.

Nevertheless, many of us put off thinking about death because we are too busy with life. Of course, in our younger years most of us think ourselves immortal. And in our preparatory twenties, apprentice thirties, and ascending forties and fifties, we are concentrating much more on life than death. For many of us it is a life of glamour and power, money and success, prestige, accumulation, and accolades. When things go well, when the children achieve, when the money is abundant and advancement assured, it's life and more life we think of, not death.

In our small way we are tempted to become like Babylon, the Roman Empire of our text. Rome too was prosperous and powerful, but also, alas, ruthless and pompous and corrupt. So in John's vision of end-time, Rome falls and meets her death. If Rome can fall, how much more ourselves. And if even Jesus meets an untimely death, how much more could we.

So what is your thinking? What do you plan to do after you die? Where will you be? What will things be like? Will it be "earth to earth, ashes to ashes, dust to dust," period, the finish, the end, finally and absolutely dead? Will your immortality be mostly in the memory of your friends? A 92-year-old member of my former church, upon hearing that explanation of immortality, said that knowing the shortness of his friends' memories, he hoped for something more than that!

Death will overtake us all, some before our time, some after our time, but all in due time will be overtaken. Ogden Nash put it whimsically when he wrote of Death, the Overtaker:

> *Said the Undertaker to the Overtaker*
> *Thank you for the butcher and the*
>   *candlestick maker,*
> *For the polo player and the*
>   *pretzel baker,*
> *For the lawyer and the lover,*
>   *and the wife-forsaker.*
> *Thank you for my bulging, verdant acre,*
> *Said the Undertaker to the Overtaker.*

Then Ogden Nash adds the ominous line: "Move in, move under, said the Overtaker." ("Tweedledee and Tweedledoom," *op.cit.* p. 281)

It happens to us all — to the undertakers who are always "the last to let you down," to the rich and famous, the powerful and prestigious, the unknown and obscure, the failures and down-and-outers. "Move in, move under, says the Overtaker" to us all, sooner or later.

II.

If death is the "great leveler" and the reminder of our common humanity and mortality, and if funerals bring us together, perhaps even more *weddings and wedding receptions unite us for celebration and the beginning of new life.*

Thankfully, that has been the case at many of our children's weddings. They have been magnetic occasions drawing us together across the miles and generations for laughter and celebration.

That was the case with our daughter's San Francisco wedding a few years ago. Great-grandchildren were there to celebrate, as were my father-in-law at age ninety, and my mother at age 84. We wondered if my mother, in failing health, would be able to endure the long flight and be active in the festivities.

But she was there in grand style, with a new dress for each part of the weekend festivities, and with an exuberance and energy that astounded us all. "Mom," we exclaimed, "aren't you tired? Do you want to rest? How do you do it all?" we asked. "It's easy," she replied. "Before I left, I asked my doctor to give me two vitamin B-12 shots instead of the usual one!" My wife and I vowed to sign up for the shots once we got home!

Wedding receptions usually are happy occasions, but there is another side to them. On the one hand, some people are *not* invited. They are left out. And on the other hand, some who are invited never show up. If wedding receptions are glad occasions for inclusiveness and a sense of oneness, they also are occasions of exclusiveness and rejection and denial. Some are in and some are out.

You may recall Jesus predicted it would be that way in the marriage feast of the Kingdom of God. In his parable of the ten maidens — five wise and five foolish — it was the five foolish who were excluded from the festivities. And in another of his famous stories, people invited to the wedding banquet of the Kingdom of God made excuses. They had purchased property, or made new investments, or were getting married so they could not come.

The insiders were too busy, too preoccupied, too self-important to accept Jesus' invitation. So he sent invitations to all the outsiders — the poor, the lame, the unsuccessful, the outcasts, and they came by the hundreds. Once again those who exalted themselves were humbled, and those who humbled themselves were exalted. We have a choice regarding our destiny.

Speaking of choices, I am reminded of a man in the back row of the church who always used to sleep through the sermons. So one Sunday the minister thought he would break him of the habit.

Very softly the minister said, "All those who want to go to heaven, stand up." The whole congregation stood up except the sleeping gentleman. The minister asked the congregation to sit down, and then said in a loud voice, "All who want to go to hell, stand up!" The sleeping man, startled, stood up, looked around, and finally said, "Well, I don't know what we are voting for, Reverend, but it looks like you and I are the only ones for it!"

Judgment does take place, even for wedding receptions, even for the ultimate wedding reception of God. If we fear the fire of ire we might also fear the ice of rejection. Robert Frost sensed it when he wrote:

> *Some say the world will end in fire,*
> *Some say in ice.*
> *From what I've tasted of desire*
> *I hold with those who favor fire.*
> *But if I had to perish twice,*
> *I think I know enough of hate*
> *To say that for destruction ice*
> *Is also great*
> *And would suffice.*
> ("Fire and Ice," *The Poems of Robert Frost*, p. 232)

Any of us who have ever been shunned by a sorority or fraternity, or any of us who have ever been blackballed by a club where we sought acceptance, or any of us who have ever been "sniffed" out of the inner circle to which we aspired, well know our world can end in ice — in the ice of refusal and rejection and the proverbial cold shoulder.

But surely God would never do such a thing, we say. Many of you no doubt read about the controversy surrounding President Clinton. No, this time it was not about his alleged sexual misconduct. This time it was about his receiving Holy Communion from the hands of a Roman Catholic priest in South Africa. Technically, only baptized Roman Catholics are admitted to Roman Catholic altars. So President Clinton, a baptized Baptist, despite former clearance with the priests in South Africa, seemed to be in violation of Church rules.

New York's Archbishop Cardinal O'Connor agreed and said so from his cathedral pulpit. While I very much disagree with the Roman Catholic doctrine of a Christian Communion Table exclusively for Roman Catholics, I very much agree with the Archbishop's position that money or prestige or power by themselves should not be the means by which one gains access to the table of God. There is judgment of those who would come to God's ultimate wedding reception, and it could be the judgment of fire or ice.

In the Bible's last book depicting the events of end-time and life after death, the risen, triumphant Christ says to the world's people, "Behold, I stand at the door and knock; if anyone hears my voice and opens the door, I will come in to him and eat with him and he with me." And the well-known painting, hanging in thousands of Sunday schools, depicts the scene with Christ knocking at the door of the cottage (which symbolizes the human heart). As you look carefully the discerning eye notes there is no handle or latch on the outside. The door to the heart must be opened from the inside. And the decision is up to us, whether or not to open our hearts to the living Christ.

But at the ultimate wedding reception in heaven, in the great welcome home banquet of life after death in the Kingdom of God, the situation is reversed. Christ is on the inside receiving all those who in faith and hope and love have longed to sup with him in the marriage feast of the Lamb of God.

And it is a beautiful scene — the scene of the ultimate wedding reception of vintage wines and gourmet foods for the soul, the scenes of glad reunions of those loved long since and lost a while, the scenes of the lame walking, the blind seeing, the deaf hearing, the mentally challenged experiencing the fullness of being, the handicapped made completely whole, the oppressed fully liberated, the suffering healed, the diseased in radiant health, the downtrodden leaping for joy in a party that goes on for centuries and centuries with exhilaration and jubilation.

John saw the vision centuries ago — the vision given him by the Easter Christ. And he wrote: "I saw the holy city, new Jerusalem, coming down out of heaven from God, prepared as a bride adorned for her husband" (Revelation 21:2). And people at the wedding reception were saying *not* let us eat, drink, and be merry, for tomorrow we *die*; *but* let us eat, drink, and be merry for we are *alive* forevermore.

And John continued to tell us what he saw:

> *And the voice from the heavenly throne said, "Behold, the dwelling of God is with (people) ... and he will wipe away every tear from their eyes, and death shall be no more, neither shall there be mourning nor crying nor pain any more, for the former things have passed away."*
> — Revelation 21:3-4

It is the grand reassurance of the Easter vision. Our dearly beloved, loved long since and lost a while, are not abandoned in cold graves and isolated niches. Their personality is not scattered and lost as so much dust in an indifferent galaxy. The powers of the universe did not bring us to life and love and creativity to end the glowing dreams in a cruel hoax of abandonment and annihilation.

No, no, not that. From the four winds, from the East and West and North and South, the Living Christ beckons all who love God to come to sit down at the great banquet feast of heaven. From all nations and tribes and peoples, from all languages and cultures and ethnic groups, from all times and places, times past and times future, he beckons to his own, "Come. To the thirsty I will give water without price from the fountain of the water of life."

So if you have eyes to see you can see them now — your brother, your husband, your parents, your child — all our beloved departed — celebrating and feasting in the ultimate wedding reception to which we all are invited.

Christ is risen!
He is risen indeed!
Alleluia! Amen!

Prayer

Eternal God, after the Palm Sunday parade and shouts of triumph, and after the Good Friday jaunts and jeers and taunts, after the nails and spear and crown of thorns and the gasping dying of our beloved Lord Jesus, we gather with you and the singing birds in the quietness of the morning near the garden tomb where they laid him. Like the women of old, we come with the guise of spices, hoping beyond all hope to behold again his powerful being and his radiating presence.

Open our eyes then to see this resurrected, transformed, beloved Son of yours, triumphant over all the powers of greed and graft, and victorious over all the forces of disease and death. Help us to behold him anew, to be open to his transforming power, and to be newly alive with his radiance.

Let him speak to us to release us from bondage and fear and to liberate us from addictive behaviors. If ours has been the negative and defensive spirit, if we have been comfortably apathetic and indifferent, if we have been gripped by the slow, gray suffocation of skepticism and cynicism — if these and other attitudes have kept us from beholding your empowering presence among us, forgive us and raise us to new life.

And for those of us who have been too much in cemeteries laying loved ones to rest, and for those of us weeping long into the lonely nights over the loss of those we loved, for all of us who mourn and grieve the power of disease and death — for us all, O God, grant the powerful assurance of resurrection to eternal life in your glorious Kingdom. And help us to know that our loved ones are safely and lovingly within your everlasting Kingdom. Through Jesus Christ our Lord. Amen.

15. Sacraments For Sometimes Secular People

Go therefore and make disciples of all nations, baptizing them in the name of the Father and of the Son and of the Holy Spirit, teaching them to observe all that I have commanded you; and lo, I am with you always, to the close of the age.
— Matthew 28:19-20

It has become customary to speak of our time as a secular age. The word secular suggests "this age" or "the present time" or "this world" as opposed to the next age or the world to come. Western culture, we are told, has centered its energies and concerns on the issues of the present life in the present world. People of our day are preoccupied with the concerns of the material, temporal world in place of serious interest in the spiritual, eternal world.

There have been numerous influences to bring us to this point. Darwin's Theory of Evolution suggested to many that our life did not have divine origin, but instead evolved out of the stuff of the universe. Astronomers and others began to question whether the universe itself had divine origins as was presupposed by the Bible. Perhaps the universe has just always existed in one form or another. If therefore neither man nor the universe have divine origin, perhaps there is no life beyond the present life. Perhaps we are deluding ourselves to think of an age and world yet to come. Possibly this is the only world and the only life there is. If so, should we not make the most of it? Many people believe so, and thus are truly secularists. That is, they believe the present age and the present life to be the only and ultimate reality.

These ideas have been buttressed by studies in the fields of psychology, sociology, anthropology, and economics. In psychology, Sigmund Freud suggested that this life was all there was and that the promise by religion of another life was largely illusion.

Indeed, in his effort to cope with the sometimes harsh realities of life, man constructs gods to lean on as crutches and develops religions in which he can take solace. The heavenly god or father is really an idealized projection of an earthly father, said Freud. When we discover the weakness and fallibility of our earthly fathers, we construct from imagination and need a heavenly father who will be immeasurably strong and infallible. Thus, for Freud, religion functioned primarily as an illusion to help us cope with the harsh realities of the present age. But for the psychologically enlightened, religion was an illusion to be abandoned as soon as we became intellectually mature.

Certain sociologists argued in a similar way. If individuals imagined and projected a god for themselves, constructed out of their weaknesses and needs, so did groups. Groups created gods and saviors and teachings which were idealized projections of what the groups thought they should be and become. Consequently, to the intellectually mature, religion was seen as a fearful and immature way of coping with life. In their view, the properly educated person abandons the illusions and escapisms of religion, the promise of a glorious age yet to come, and concentrates on this life as being the one and only life.

It did not take long for economics, politics, and anthropology to follow suit. Economic forces and dialectical materialism really determine the destinies of peoples, said Karl Marx. Religion functions largely as an opiate to keep people drugged with a futile hope for a better life to come. Thus Communism attempted to awaken people from their otherworldly stupor to seize the present age by revolting against the rich and propertied classes to bring in the day of the proletariat, the working classes. Religion was for old women too advanced to own up to their grand deception.

Of course capitalism has much the same philosophical premise — namely, the affirmation of this world as the only *real* world, and therefore the one in which we should expend our energies and upon which we should fasten our hope. The politics of both Communism and Capitalism function much the same way, affirming this age as the only age. The city of man is not, as in Saint Augustine, a foretaste and copy of the City of God. It has no obligation to another reality. This world and these cities are the only realities. All else is illusion.

Next, it was only natural that theology and anthropology would change places. If theology was the study of God and anthropology the study of man, it was now natural to say that anthropology was theology. Since man creates gods in his image, and not vice versa, it was natural to conclude that the proper study of God was man.

Thus in our time, the thrust of centuries of teaching was turned upside down. If in the Middle Ages, people were concerned about immortality and saving their souls, in our time they are concerned about good health and good life here and now. If in centuries past, people were solicitous as to how they might please God, in our time, they are solicitous as to how they might please themselves. If people of the past were future oriented, people today are oriented toward the *now*. We have little faith in life to come. We want to experience it now, since as secularists, we conclude this is the only life.

I.

It is in this context we speak of sacraments — sacraments for a sometimes-secular people, or sacraments for a people who are secular all the time.

The word "sacrament" comes from the Latin, *sacramentum* which means "to bind oneself to another in solemn oath." At the outset, we secular people have no real problem with that since we participate in a number of solemn oaths throughout our lives, from pledging a fraternity, to signing a mortgage, to saying marriage vows, to signing contracts.

But, of course, sacrament implies more than that in the religious context. It suggests God and man binding themselves to one another in solemn oath. Thus a sacrament is an oath or covenant or contract between God and man which includes obligations and benefits. More than that, in religious circles, sacraments function as a means of grace by which God mediates his gifts and favor. Thus sacraments are agents or symbols of the divine. They are meant to be expressions of the divine, a way of participating in the divine.

The Church of the Middle Ages established seven sacraments: baptism, confirmation, communion, holy orders, marriage, penance, and extreme unction. Through the ministration of these rites, the grace and saving presence of God was said to be mediated. By participating in these, people participated in the reality of the divine and were assured of eternal life in the age to come.

The Protestant Reformation of the sixteenth century reduced the number to two — baptism and communion. Although most Protestants practice the other five in some form — confirmation, ordination, marriage, penance, and extreme unction — they call them holy rites or sacred acts rather than sacraments. Whether two or seven, the sacraments have been understood as means of the divine grace.

II.

Consider baptism. Baptism has had a long history in both biblical and non-biblical religions. Several of the mystery religions in the Graeco-Roman world used baptism as a means of cleansing and of initiation into the divine mysteries. Ancient Jews used proselyte baptism as a means of cleansing and initiation for converts to Judaism. John the Baptist was baptizing in the River Jordan, using it as a rite of moral and spiritual cleansing to prepare people for the coming Kingdom of God. Later, as in the Great Commission, Jesus commanded his disciples to teach, preach, and to baptize. Thus the Christian Church has practiced baptism in response to both Jesus' example and his command.

The Greek word, *baptizo*, means "to dip, plunge, or immerse." Jesus and early Christians most likely were immersed in water in fulfillment of the command of Jesus. As in other ancient religions, so in Christianity, baptism was a moral and spiritual cleansing, a rite of initiation into the divine mysteries and into the divine community. It was an outward, visible act, signifying an inward conversion or change of life. Baptism signified a change in loyalties. It was the "swearing in" ceremony of the army of God.

This is amply expressed in Paul's letter to the Romans. For him, baptism is an apt reenactment of the death, burial, and resurrection of Jesus. On the cross, Jesus crucified all his Messianic aspirations, all his hope for being a Jewish hero and savior, all his dreams of being the new David, or the Jewish Alexander the Great. On the cross he put to death the age-old urge of man to make of himself a god. In the crucifixion, he faced once for all the powerful argument that *this* world is all there is, that *this* age is the only age that counts, that *this* is the one and only life which one must save at all costs.

On the cross, he finally had to practice what he had been preaching, namely, that he who saves his life will lose it, but he who loses his life for God will find it. On the cross, he had to let go the fantastic promise of success the world held for him, the tantalizing prospect that he could restore the Kingdom of David, the alluring challenge of the wilderness temptation that the world could be his.

Like the first Adam, Jesus also was tempted to take a bite out of the big apple, to believe in himself that he could go it alone, that he could, in some way, establish his own immortality. But on the cross, he vowed again his faith in God and his allegiance to God's will. On the cross the arrogance and rebellion of the first Adam resounded within his inmost being, and he knew he must affirm the will of God over the will of man, even though it meant suffering and death.

On the cross, Jesus bet his life on God and won, for God vindicated him in the resurrection, putting his stamp of approval upon him for the beginning of a new mankind. By reversing the arrogance and conceit of the first Adam who declared himself self-sufficient in a secular world where he would create his own paradise, Jesus, of all people, confessed his lack of self-sufficiency for building the Kingdom of God, and affirmed his ultimate faith in God rather than himself.

Therefore, at the very heart of the Christian faith is the denial of the ultimate reality of secularism and non-theistic humanism. Even Jesus, the most admirable man we have known, would not claim himself the all-sufficient reality. God alone is good, said Jesus. He alone has the promise of the ultimate life, the true life which is life indeed.

Christian baptism is a symbol of this central event of the Christian faith. As the believer comes to the point of decision, he is crucified on a cross; that is, all his messianic expectations, all his dreams of success and fame, all his assurances of immortality, that is, making a name for himself, all his pretensions of self-sufficiency and ego-centricity — all these are crucified, put to death, in the act of faith of confessing God as God and Christ as Christ and himself as only a mortal man.

Then, as Christ was buried in the earth, so the believer is submerged in the grave of water, to cleanse him and to sever his ultimate tie to the world of time and sense as the only reality, in order to come alive to the time and eternal reality of God. And just as Jesus was raised from the tomb to new and eternal life, so the believer is raised from the tomb of baptism to participate in eternal life, that is, to live in this world, but not of it; to serve in this world in anticipation of the world to come.

In baptism, the ultimate fear and enemy of secularism is overcome — the enemy of death. Whereas once we were convinced that if we did not make it in this world, we would have no life at all, we now become convinced that this world is illusion, that what is seen is temporal, but that what is unseen is eternal. Thus, in the sacrament of baptism, the world is turned upside down again, and by the grace of God, we see that theology is anthropology. God is the primary reality. Man is derivative, not vice versa. God creates man and then re-creates him in his image. That is the true reality, the divine mystery conveyed to us in the sacrament, in place of the earlier presumption that God was created in our image and thus under our control.

Therefore, at its very heart, baptism stands in contradiction to the teachings of the secular age. By it, the Christian community bears witness to the higher reality and the nobler allegiance. Through it we affirm the grace of God and participation in the divine mystery which promises victory over sin and death.

True, the mode of baptism has varied between immersion, sprinkling, and pouring. Yes, we have had arguments as to whether infants would be baptized. But the overarching meaning is that in baptism we become a new people, following the New Man, the New Adam, into the promise of eternal life, experienced now, and in the age to come.

III.

Consider the second sacrament of Protestantism, that of *Communion* or the Lord's Supper or the Eucharist.

If baptism is the rite of cleansing and initiation into the community of the divine, communion is the rite of spiritual sustenance of the holy community; that is, the community devoted to the reality of God over the reality of the present age. If baptism marks the entrance into the army of the Lord, communion represents the holy food by which the army is sustained.

The origins of this sacrament are to be found in the supper Jesus shared with his twelve disciples on the last night of his life. The Last Supper drew upon the Jewish Seder or Passover Feast which recalled the exodus of the ancient Hebrews from Egypt, their land of bondage and death, toward the Promised Land of liberty and life. Thus the Lord's Supper or Communion has aptly come to be the feast symbolizing liberation not from Egypt, but from death itself, and our progress toward the Promised Land, which this time is not Palestine but heaven.

More than that, the Communion bread is seen as the divine manna of the Wilderness Wandering which sustained the ancient Hebrews on their way to their land of promise. And the water out of the rock is symbolized by the wine which is the drink sustaining us for the life which is eternal and in the Promised Land of heaven. Theologians of the early Church often called the bread and wine the food of immortality. Even John's Gospel says if we eat the bread and drink the wine, we have eternal life within us already.

Christians keep the sacrament of Communion because Jesus asked us to and because the early Church set the example for succeeding ages. Indeed, the earliest church in Jerusalem may have celebrated Communion daily in their homes with one another during the course of the regular meal. Later, in other parts of the world, the Communion was observed during love feasts, the first century equivalent of our fellowship dinners. During the love feast, when the bread was broken, it was done in memory of Christ, and in the same mood, the wine was shared.

In the letter of First Corinthians, we see that the Corinthian Christians began to abuse Communion and the love feast. Some would come early and begin to eat and drink, so that by the time others got there, some were even drunk. The rich tended to have more to eat and drink, so that the poor were made envious and embarrassed.

Thus, the Communion in Corinth began to be a feast of the secular mind rather than the sacred. The emphasis was upon me and mine and having it all now, rather than upon waiting and sharing with all. Instead of eating and drinking toward the higher reality of the eternal Kingdom yet to come, they ate and drank satisfaction for themselves only in the here and now. Thus in place of being a means of divine grace, it became a means of putting hostile space between believers. Consequently, they were eating and drinking judgment upon themselves, said Paul.

Over the years the Communion was taken out of the home and fellowship hall and placed on the high altar of the church. More and more as the bread and wine were consecrated they spoke of the repeated sacrifice of the body of Christ. Eventually by the Middle Ages, in the ritual of the Mass, the bread and wine actually became the body and blood of our Lord. Thus the doctrine of transubstantiation. Bread and wine were changed in substance to body and blood. Therefore, the believer, as in the ancient mystery religions, participated in a kind of divine cannibalism, eating the divine body with its life-giving power, thus ensuring the participant of divine and eternal life. It was indeed the food and drink of immortality, the ultimate victory over the grip of the presumptuous secular age.

Of course the Protestant Reformers thought the doctrine of the Mass excessive and mistaken. For them the bread and wine were symbols of the divine reality, representations of it, not the actual flesh and blood of the Jesus of history. Lutherans spoke of the real presence of Christ in the elements, Christ *with* and *in* the elements and thus consubstantiation. Calvinists and Zwinglians, who were Congregational, Presbyterian, and Reformed Church forbears, went further to say the elements were indeed symbols, but symbols which served as a memorial to a sacrifice made once for all. Thus, the emphasis turned away from the elements to the acts of eating and drinking together in memory of Christ. But if Roman Catholics erred on the side of divine cannibalism, Calvinists erred on the side of a barren, sterile, rationalistic, memorial feast.

Nevertheless, perhaps the real significance is in the act of faith implied in eating and drinking together, not only in memory of Christ, but in anticipation of his coming again in glory. The Christian Community, by observing this sacrament bears witness to the judgment of God upon our secular pretensions and arrogance, and says Sunday after Sunday that we are a community believing toward the Age to Come.

By the bread and wine, we are reminded not only of Christ's Crucifixion, that is, his death to the beguilement of this age, but our own crucifixion. By eating and drinking together as a Christian family around a common table recalling common stories which form our identity, we nurture one another in living the resurrection life, proclaiming the validity and power of the Lord's death and resurrection until he comes again.

It is this kind of faith, this kind of eating and drinking that distinguishes Communion from other feasts. As Paul says, if there is no resurrection, let us eat, drink, and be merry with the best this world has to offer, for tomorrow we die. Let us pull out all the stops for making it in this life if there is no life to come. Let us make our Camelot and heaven and Promised Land in the here and now if there is no real promise of life after death.

Nevertheless, the sacrament of Communion is a means of divine grace because it continues to bear witness to the reality of God and the promise of the life which is life indeed. No wonder it was the center of worship for centuries and still is in most churches. Protestant churches have mistakenly relegated communion to just a few Sundays, making preaching more or less their central sacrament. We need to re-examine our practice and consider restoring communion to at least monthly, if not weekly, observance.

Yes, I suppose Christians will continue to argue about the precise meaning of Baptism and Communion. Yes, I suppose rationalists and secularists will continue to ridicule the idea of these sacraments being a means of divine grace.

But there is a sense in which all the world is sacramental, testifying to realities beyond our usual apprehension, bearing witness to presences and truths only glimpsed in the passing scene, but apprehended by the depths of mind and soul where deep calls to deep.

So it is, these sacraments stand as testimonies that, ultimately, we do not belong to this age, nor the present order of things. They stand as symbols, bearers of the divine reality, agents of truth which empower us, but which we cannot grasp or possess, that we ultimately belong to the Heavenly Father, and that there is indeed a final Promised Land.

No wonder Jesus' pictures of life after death were not solemn and morbid. They were not a dark, grey Jewish Sheol or pit, or Platonic nether world of disembodied souls. Instead, his pictures were of feasts and parties and banquets — times of joy and gladness and happy reunions. And greatest of all would be the marriage supper of the Lamb of God, where all Christ's people share in the ultimate victory banquet of our Lord. It will be, at long last, paradise regained, at long last the victory of the age to come.

Thus with the hymn we sing:

> *O blest communion, fellowship divine!*
> *We feebly struggle, they in glory shine;*
> *Yet all are one in thee, for all are thine,*
> *Alleluia, Alleluia.*
>
> *And when the strife is fierce, the warfare long,*
> *Steals on the ear, the distant triumph song,*
> *And hearts are brave again, and arms are strong,*
> *Alleluia, Alleluia.*
>   ("For All The Saints Who From Their Labors Rest,"
>   William Washam How, 1864)

Prayer

Eternal God, whose thought and presence permeate the universe faster than the speed of light, but whose grace and mercy wait patiently for the openness of the slowest heart and mind, we worship and adore you because we cannot help ourselves. The wonders of the world are too overwhelming not to offer praise. The mysteries of life are too perplexing not to seek your guidance. The tragedies of our existence are too devastating and the victories too exhilarating for us not to be conscious of your genius and power and presence in all the world. Wonderfully and fearfully have we been made. In reverence and awe we acknowledge you as Creator and Lord. Praise be to you, O God.

Nevertheless, in spite of our awe and praise, we would be less than honest if we did not confess our frequent doubt. You seem so often an absent God, distant and uncaring. For all our praise of your power and glory, we do our share of questioning about your love and mercy, about your willingness to hear the anguish of our souls and to heal with compassion the brokenness of our lives. We want to believe you are present among us. Help thou our unbelief.

You know us well, O Lord, and readily perceive how we seek after power and glory to compensate for our anxieties of insignificance. We crave attention and notoriety, we long for the power and deference which wealth bestows, we grasp for the advantage of the upper hand, and strive to be near the limelight of the celebrity circle.

Help us see again our strenuous efforts to overcome our anxieties and fears by manufacturing our own sense of power and glory and divine significance. If we are anxious over an inadequate background, save us from the freneticism by which we would presume to lift ourselves into your presence. If ours is the fear of being left out or rejected, save us from the futility of moral compromise in an effort to win an empty companionship. If in mid-life it has dawned upon us that we never before have come to terms with ourselves or with you, save us from the silliness of pursuing the ever-evasive fountain of youth. If ours has been the smug, provincial life, newly awakened by culture shock to larger realities, keep us from the vain pursuit of your real presence in any place or thing. If in human loves we have been transfixed, grant that we may see them as symbols and sacraments of your abiding presence in a sometimes vacant world.

O Eternal God of the universe, whose will it is that we should know you as loving Father, and whose desire it is that we should come to know your mind and will and experience your love; grant that we might be open to you, to make our hearts and minds the very temple of your loving presence. Cleanse us of all unrighteousness. Destroy these idols of the soul to which we cling for temporal security. Release us from the clutter and clamor which detract from your still, small voice which speaks gently to us, assuring us you are with us always, even to the end of the world and beyond. Through Jesus Christ our Lord. Amen.

16. Eating And Drinking Toward Spiritual Health

For anyone who eats and drinks without discerning the body eats and drinks judgment upon himself. That is why many of you are weak and ill, and some have died. — 1 Corinthians 11:29-30

Eating and drinking are two of the most necessary and enjoyable activities of the human experience. Most always we have feelings of pleasure and delight, camaraderie and satisfaction, when we think of these basic acts of eating and drinking. Whether it be at our mother's table or our wife's, or at a favorite restaurant or at the home of a friend who is a good cook, the acts of eating and drinking conjure up some of our fondest memories.

I remember a few years ago when vitamins first were popular, there were predictions that some day pills would entirely replace conventional food. Want a steak for dinner? Take a steak pill. Want a salad? Take a salad pill. Like a dessert? Take an ice cream and cake pill. Those predictions never came true of course, for we enjoy too much the immense variety of taste, texture, smell, and satisfaction associated with good food.

Consequently, cookbooks flourish, restaurants capture us with their specialties, gourmet magazines and newspaper food recipes and reviews abound, and businessmen and advertisers constantly are dreaming up new ways to entice our taste buds. If it is true that an army marches as much on its stomach as it does on its feet, and if it is true that the way to a man's heart is through his stomach, it may also be true that many societies live from one meal to the next. Not only is eating and drinking necessary, we love it.

We love it because it is more than a physical act. A rabbi speaking at our church was asked, why is it Jews are known for their good food? Well, for one thing, he quipped, persecution has put them in many parts of the world, and they have picked up good recipes wherever they have been! But more than that, for a good Jewish mother, food is love, and love is food. In times of illness, good chicken soup is more than soup — it is warm, tangible, tasty love!

Well, today we long for both love and good food and at times both seem plenty hard to find. True, we eat a lot, some of us too much. And many of us are big on health foods or special diets. Others are concerned about preservatives, additives, and carcinogens in our food. So most of us relish pure food, cooked from scratch, served with love among family and friends. It is not quite true, of course, to say we are what we eat, for Albert Einstein and many an idiot have eaten essentially the same foods. But good eating habits obviously do contribute to better health.

There is physical food and drink, but there also is food for mind and spirit. Librarians are fond of saying you are what you read. But that again is only half true because many people presumably read many of the same books Abraham Lincoln read, and yet there was only one Lincoln. Nevertheless, food and drink for mind and spirit are as essential for health and wholeness as are food and drink for body. It is the mental and spiritual diet that largely distinguishes human beings from other physical creatures. We are what we are not only because we can eat and drink, but also because we can read and think, love and believe and decide. And just as what we ingest into the physical body affects our physical health, so too, what we ingest into our spiritual and mental being affects our spiritual health.

So what have we been reading lately besides sex and violence? Anything on philosophy or ethics? Anything on history or morals? Anything about love and prayer, God and Jesus? Anything about a sensible Christian family life? And have we been doing any spiritual exercises lately? Many of us are into jogging, but how about deep knee bends for prayer? Many are into tennis, but is anyone for hitting out against injustice or organized evil?

Paul said that if bodily exercise is profitable for little, then spiritual exercise is profitable for much. If bodily exercise tends to prolong physical life, then spiritual exercise develops the soul for eternity.

But in our text, Paul warns against a practice that is bringing harm to Christians — it is the practice of observing the Communion in an inappropriate manner. Consequently, he advises them, and us, on ways in which we can eat and drink ourselves toward spiritual health.

I.

In the first place, when we come to the Communion, *we should come with a sense of thanksgiving.*

One common and historic word for the Communion is Eucharist, which comes from the Greek word, *eucharisteo*, which means to give thanks. In the night in which he was betrayed, Jesus took bread and gave thanks. Thus for many Christians, Communion has come to be known as the feast of thanksgiving.

Thanksgiving is an essential ingredient for spiritual health, especially in our day when we are so obsessed with greed, so concerned with getting and having, with moving on to more rather than giving thanks for what has been received.

At Christ's table we give thanks not for what we have *achieved*, but for what we have *received*. If at our family tables we think our bread is the work of our hands alone, we have to look farther, to the deeper miracle of life, to the miracle of seed bearing seed, to the wonder of seedtime and harvest. All we do is manipulate and process the life that is given by God in the harvest.

Likewise at the table of our Lord, we give thanks not so much that we have built a church, carved a table, and put bread and wine on it. Rather, we give thanks that Christ has invited us to be his own, that he has called us into his kingdom to share in the gifts of salvation.

And how has that invitation come? Not by our hands, but through the hands of faith that have preceded us. The majority of us did not receive our faith first of all at our present church. Somewhere else it was given by parents and teachers, who in turn received it from previous generations, on back to Christ himself. Consequently, we are at the table not so much by what we have achieved, but by what we have received from the patient faith and suffering love of previous generations, from prophets and apostles, missionaries and scholars and martyrs.

The great acts of life and salvation have not been wrought by our own hands so much as by the hands of God. Therefore we come to the table to rest from our fevered pace, to set our troubled minds at rest, to be absorbed in the larger act of thanksgiving, to be cleansed from the anxiety of greed and the distorted demands of pride. The true act of thanksgiving humbles us, causing us to acknowledge how much we are blessed beyond our deserving, beyond the labors of our hands.

II.

Another attitude essential for eating and drinking toward spiritual health is confession.

It is not popular to make confession of sins in religious services today. Many people who will pay hundreds or thousands of dollars to a psychologist or psychiatrist to confess guilt and wrongdoing will refuse to come to church to come clean with God. Others speak of their weekly session with their analyst or psychiatrist, as some people used to speak of going to weekly religious confession. And of course, many others have enjoyed making public confession in books and magazines. As someone has quipped, in Washington, D.C., confession is not only good for the soul; it could turn out to be a best seller!

Confession is the admission of our unworthiness. In the presence of important people, we often go through a ritual act of cleansing and confession, thereby acknowledging our sense of unworthiness.

For example, one woman told of her experience meeting the President of the United States. She went through elaborate bathing and grooming procedures. Her hair was especially coifed; her dress was the finest. In every way she was sensing her unworthiness to meet the President and was attempting to make herself presentable. I wish we might come to Communion with as great a concern. Regrettably, many of us come to Christ's table in a far more slip-shod manner. Slovenly at times, inattentive, sullen, insensitive, even boorish, we fail to receive his presence because we are not ready to receive it. Many of us are too arrogant in spirit, too hard, too prideful, too anxious to receive the spiritual food he has to give for our spiritual health.

Great coaches can do little with athletes who know it all. Great teachers of music make little progress with students who presume themselves better than they are. College professors make little headway with students who are inflated beyond reality. Humility and a teachable spirit are essential for success and health in all disciplines, including religion.

We all are unworthy. We have not been invited to the table because we are the world's most beautiful people. We have not received invitations because Christ wants to gather all the good people for a mutual admiration society. Instead, we come confessing we are not worthy to sit at the feet of so great a master.

III.

The third attitude essential for spiritual health is the cultivation of a sense of community.

It was especially here that the Corinthian Christians failed. In their day, about 54 A.D., Communion was still held in conjunction with a love feast. A love feast was the rough equivalent of our fellowship suppers. The Corinthian Christians would each bring their baskets of food and wine, but it got so many would eat and drink before the others arrived. In fact, some drank so much they became tipsy!

Consequently, the very intent of the love feast was shattered by the selfishness and thoughtlessness of the few. And when it came time to break their bread in memory of Christ, many had already eaten and now were loud and boisterous. And when it was time to share the wine in memory of Christ's lifeblood, some already had confiscated their supply and were a bit drunken. Paul sternly reminded them that if they wanted to have a private dinner party, they should do that at home. But when they come to the Lord's Table, they should be concerned about one another and share what they have.

It is important to remember that when we go to a dinner party with friends, we must relax into the host's hospitality. Who of us would go in a superior spirit, thinking to presume upon our host's graciousness by taking charge and by showing him how things ought to be done? Such arrogance of spirit is not only bad manners; it violates a sense of community with our host and the other invited guests. Instead, when accepting an invitation, we go to receive, not to achieve. We go to share with thanksgiving the favor and presence of a friend.

Likewise, at the table of Christ. We come because he has invited us. We would not come in arrogance, presuming upon his good favor by telling him how things ought to be done, or how fortunate he is to have us there. We come in humility, ready to receive with thanksgiving the food and presence of our host and his other guests whom he loves.

While Communion is a private matter between us and our host, it also is a community matter between our host and all of us. Just as at a dinner party we do not have the host all to ourselves, so at Christ's table we all share his presence. He is not our private possession. We commune with him and with one another. Thus rather than splitting us and the world apart, Christ, at his table, would bring us all together to be harmonious and peaceable, building one another up in love.

Paul gives warning to the Corinthian Christians who think only of themselves, who do not discern the body, his Church. By our selfishness, arrogance, and ingratitude we fracture the oneness and wholeness intended for the Church and the world.

How can we make headway against the spiritual diseases of our time? Against the disease of neuroses and guilt, depression and boredom, narrowness of mind and hardness of heart? By coming to the Communion table with thanksgiving for God's patience and grace; by unburdening ourselves through honest confession; and by having concern for one another, by caring, by building up the community of faith.

Prayer

Eternal God, who fills the world with all good things and who sustains your creatures, both great and small, with the earth's bounty, we praise you for all the good we receive at your hand. We plant the seed and cultivate, fertilize, and harvest, but it is you, O Lord, who through the ongoing miracle of growth, gives the increase. Make us aware again that we are agents of life, not its creators. Cause us to remember that without the promise of seed bearing seed after its kind, the labor of our callused hands would be as nothing.

But we have more than bodies to feed. In the depths of our beings we hunger and thirst after you. With our deep freezer full, we discover an inward hunger our daily bread cannot fill. Drinking from our abundant wells, we discover thirst again and again. We come to you to seek the living water and the bread of life.

Take then these sometimes impoverished souls of ours, and fill them with new meaning and purpose. When the routine of abundance hardens our hearts, awaken us to gratitude and thanksgiving. When the glitter of this world's gold captures our affection and allegiance, by your mercy, lure us to yourself again, that we may distinguish between ephemeral fool's gold, and true gold which is life indeed.

Speak then to the emptiness of each of us. Fill those depressed with a new sense of hope. For those exhausted in grief and wasted in remorse and regret, infuse with strength and courage to begin again. For those hardened by cynicism and evil, plant seeds of hope and faith which will spring forth like new life in the crevices of rocks. And for those parched and brown by the blistering heat of this world's suffering and evil, grant a full measure of your refreshing presence, so that like the new growth of spring they may come to life again, radiant and green.

Fill us then, O Lord, with your grace and Spirit, for the abundance of this world's good leave us empty still. Amen.

17. The Bread Of Life

Jesus said to them, "I am the bread of life; he who comes to me shall not hunger, and he who believes in me shall never thirst." — John 6:35

Compared to the Palestine of Jesus' day, America is a veritable paradise of physical comfort and a bountiful land overflowing with milk and honey. If a first century Galilean peasant farmer could see the amber fields of waving grain on America's Great Plains, he surely would think he had died and gone to heaven, or that the Messianic Age had arrived in all its glory and splendour. Or if he could watch the huge freighters at Duluth, Minnesota, being loaded with ton after ton of golden grain, he would rightly think he would never again have to worry about his daily bread.

Think of it. If only a few years ago our population was seventy percent agrarian, now only three or four percent of our population provides food not only for us, but for much of the world. America is indeed the breadbasket of the world, and few of us ever seriously worry about our daily bread.

Indeed, our worry is not about daily bread, but daily diet. Doctors, food nutritionists, and authors have made millions on advising how to cut down on our intake of daily bread. Exercise programs from jogging to swimming to weight lifting have been devised to help us burn off the calories. We worry not so much about the availability of food, but about how well it is prepared.

Not only would the Galilean farmer of Jesus' time be amazed at our abundance; so would most of the people of history. Visit the ruins of ancient Greece or walk in the banqueting halls of medieval kings, and it will become apparent that most Americans live far better than royalty of the past. We are better dressed, better clothed and housed, better transported, and in many ways healthier than the majority of people of history.

Bread, you say? Bread for living? Prosperity and affluence for living? We have it and have it in abundance.

Therefore, perhaps this story of Jesus and the feeding of the 5,000 and their subsequent search for more bread is especially significant for us. For if Jesus could urge those first-century peasants to search for the bread of life which gives life indeed, how much more might he urge us, in all our abundance, to look beyond the physical bread to the spiritual food which nourishes the soul toward eternal life.

I.

Look again at the setting. On the previous day Jesus had fed the 5,000 by encouraging them to open up and share what they had, rather then hoarding it for themselves. They all had brought breadbaskets for the day, but were afraid to open them fearing there would not be enough for them and their neighbors. But following Jesus' example, they opened both their hearts and their baskets and there was food left over.

Eventually Jesus and his disciples crossed the Sea of Galilee to Capernaum and the next day the crowd followed. They were amazed at his teachings but also impressed with the miracle of the feeding and were now looking for another free meal. They dreamed of a Messiah who would care for their physical needs without personal toil.

Most all of us are looking for a free meal just as those Galilean peasants used to. Even well off people are always looking for a free lunch. For example, I once belonged to a club which gave away, by drawing, free hams and turkeys three times a year. Attendance at club meetings tripled on those days, because those well-dressed, well-paid business and professional men, who could well afford turkeys and hams, hoped to win a free meal. So it was with those peasants who had just had a free meal at Jesus' feeding of the 5,000. No wonder they looked for him the next day. It sure beat working.

Jesus understood, of course, their physical hunger and needs, but he was disappointed they had not looked beyond to their deeper, spiritual, intellectual, emotional needs, which his teachings could satisfy. As Jesus said to them. "You seek me, not because you saw signs, but because you ate your fill of the loaves." And he went on to make his point: "Do not labor for the food which perishes, but for the food which endures to eternal life, which the Son of man will give to you ..." (John 6:27).

Jesus knew, as we all know, that after the body has been fed, there remains a hunger of the soul, which only food for the soul can satisfy. Jesus knew that what truly gives us zest for living is not just well-stocked deep freezes and full stomachs, but a heart and mind full of purpose for living and a philosophy of life which inspires the heart and mind toward their eternal goal.

The ancient Romans, in their power and prosperity, often could find nothing else to do but to stuff themselves at feasts, go outside and use an emetic, and then go stuff themselves again. Through gluttony and drunkenness they presumed to find life. Through overindulgence in bread, they presumed to have arrived at the pinnacle of human experience. But as Matthew Arnold put it:

> *In his cool hall with haggard eyes,*
> *the Roman noble lay;*
> *He drove abroad in furious guise*
> *Along the Appian Way;*
> *He made a feast, drank fierce and fast;*
> *He crowned his hair with flowers;*
> *No easier nor no quicker passes*
> *The impracticable hours.*

The Roman noble has his counterpart in many contemporary Americans who go from feast to feast to forestall a satiated dreariness and blasé boredom. We often have bread in abundance, but not the Bread of Life.

The truth is that life is more than food and drink. Or as Paul put it, the Kingdom of God does not consist of food and drink but of peace and joy in the Holy Spirit and in power (Romans 14:17). Well-fed, we seek, nevertheless, for food for the mind and soul.

II.

But bread is not just a matter of banqueting. It has to do with how we organize our lives.

Consider the ways in which we imitate the peasants of Galilee in seeking physical bread more than spiritual, in laboring for bread which perishes, in place of food which endures to eternal life.

Our higher educational system is largely designed to prepare people to earn a good living — and it should do that, of course. But at the same time, courses in philosophy and theology and literature and psychology often are avoided. We tend to be strong on the practical, but weak on the philosophical and specialize and intensify our abilities to make bread, but minimize or neglect the questions of *why* we live or for *what* we live. We know well how to provide for the health and comfort of the physical body, but often avoid or neglect the health and well being of the mind and soul.

Consider, too, our personal and family life. Most of us live reasonably well, strive to make sure our children eat properly, sleep and exercise well, dress appropriately, and behave in a manner suitable to our lifestyle. But we too easily neglect discussions of spiritual matters at home. We shy away from family prayer or Bible reading. Church is forsaken for physical pleasure. Philosophical and theological questions are avoided. Personal feelings are neglected or thwarted and we feel lonely or bored or depressed or ignored. While physical bread and comfort are important and essential, we often forget that spiritual bread and nourishment are even more important and infuse our daily lives with meaning and purpose.

Or consider our economic and political systems. C. G. Jung, the well-known psychoanalyst, has written that "a clever European is convinced that religion and such things are good enough for the masses and for women, but are of little weight compared to economic and political affairs" (*Man in Search of a Soul*, p. 252, quoted in *Interpreter's Bible*, Vol. 8, p. 563).

Of course politics and economics are important for providing our daily bread. But eventually cultures must ask why they exist and what ultimate values undergird their political and economic system. Totalitarian regimes exploit the masses and oppress the individual. But when the gospel of Jesus and the high sense of individual worth and dignity of man taught by Paul come into play, the deeper questions of economics and politics are raised.

Oppressive political systems want to avoid revolutionary ideas of freedom and private property and individual initiative and incentive. Ancient Rome gave the masses bread and circuses so as to forestall the deeper questions regarding the true life for all people. Oppressive regimes in every century usually are pleased to have religion as an opiate or sedative or tranquilizer or rationalizer of the *status quo*. But they rightly fear the revolutionary message of Jesus which has to do with the soul and spirit of human beings, not just their bodies and bellies. Most economic and political systems want us to concentrate on working only for the bread that perishes. Jesus forever calls us to the larger question of working for the bread which gives eternal life, life with purpose and meaning, here and forever.

III.

But finally the question of the Bread of Life comes down to you and me personally. Very often we fall into the trap of wanting to *use* religion to acquire free bread or to accomplish our own goals and purposes, rather than have religion be the means whereby we submit our minds and wills and lives to be used for God's goals and purposes. Like the Galilean peasants, we want Jesus to submit to us rather than submit ourselves to him to be used by him.

But it is in that submission, in that faith, that we find the Bread of Life. The Galileans asked Jesus what work they should do to acquire the Bread of Life. He replied that the Bread of Life was a gift of God's grace which could be attained only through the "work" of faith, through the "work" of believing in him. We are to have faith in him for the eternal life, rather than just the temporal. We are to work toward the qualitative life, not just the quantitative. We are to realize that life does not consist in the abundance of our possessions but in the knowledge of God's love and grace. While we do live by bread, we do not live by bread alone, but by the Word which proceeds out of the mouth of God.

In his book, *Man in Search of a Soul*, psychoanalyst C. G. Jung has written that of the many, many people he has counseled from all over the world, one of the basic needs he uncovered was that of "finding a religious outlook on life." That was especially true of people over 35. And said Dr. Jung, "none of them has been really healed who did not regain his religious outlook" (p. 264, quoted in *Interpreter's Bible*, Vol. 8, p. 564).

Jesus was calling the Galileans to decide then and there for God's Kingdom. It was already present among them. The manna from heaven which they expected in the Messianic Age was coming down in the teachings and person of Jesus. By believing in him as God's Son with God's stamp of approval, they would find bread for their souls which would feed them for eternal life. By believing in him, they would find those deep meanings of life, and be infused with the confidence that life was not futile, but was coming to a glorious climax in the banquet feast of God for all who believed.

And so it is today, through the agency of the Church, Jesus is calling not the ancient Galileans, but us. The manna, the Bread of Heaven, the Bread of Life has come and is coming. But it is required of us to partake of it in faith, to believe on Jesus as God's unique Son through whom we receive not only the gift of a life full of meaning and purpose now, but through whom we also receive the gift of life everlasting.

Lord, we believe. Help thou our unbelief.

Prayer

O Eternal God, our Father, who has so ordained the world that birds of the air find food for their young, and the children of men receive sustenance from the beauty of the earth; we praise you for the mystery and miracle of life. We thank you for the fecundity of the earth, for life-giving food bursting forth in green fields and fruit-laden orchards. Praise be to you for a well-ordered world wherein we receive our daily bread.

Nevertheless, we are conscious of those millions of our fellows malnourished and underfed. We pray for the poor and destitute in our land and lands abroad that the hungry might be fed and that the thirsty might have drink. We pray for reform in political and economic systems, which oppress people and breed poverty. We pray inspiration for researchers that new crops and methods might ensue for hunger-stricken nations. Show us new ways politically and economically to share and distribute the surplus we often enjoy. Well-sustained in daily bread, open our hearts to those less fortunate, and grant us wisdom and strength to share.

But life is more than meat and drink. How often, O Lord, we have come to prosperity and yet have felt empty, as though we had missed something along life's way. Well-fed and sometimes overnourished in body, there often remains a hunger of the soul, a longing of the mind and heart for food not of this world.

Loving Father, whose promise and pleasure it is to nourish those who come to you in faith, fill us today with insight into ourselves and your purposes for our lives. If we have been wayward and wanton, by your mercy, call us back to your banquet table of grace and love. If we have been willful and stubborn, deliver us from the stale breads of our intellectual sustenance to feast upon the Living Bread. If like medieval kings we pride ourselves upon the dainty morsels of our manufacture but neglect the solid food of your eternal word, call us to repentance and to the nutrition which gives life eternal. If we have grown content with material satiation and are bloated with the conceit of this life, awaken us anew to your Eternal Kingdom and puncture our pride that we may again enter the narrow gate into your banquet of life. Through Jesus Christ our Lord. Amen.

18. Water And The Thirst For Life

O God, thou art my God, I seek thee, my soul thirsts for thee; my flesh faints for thee, as in a dry and weary land where no water is. — Psalm 63:1

In the beginning there was no water, says scientist John Stewart Collis. Nor was there any earth, strictly speaking. There was only fire. As the fire cooled, molten liquid turned into a solid crust of rock on the earth's surface. This cooling process let off vast amounts of vapors which formed an atmosphere that contained all the oceans and lakes, rivers and streams of earth.

Then the water fell to the hot earth in torrents of rivers and oceans and the hot and barren rocks threw it back again. Aeons and aeons the battle raged between water and fire, rain and volcanoes, until water won and covered the whole earth.

But fire could not be contained beneath the oceans and hardened crust of earth. It burst forth in gigantic volcanic action to produce continents and mountain ranges. Deep crevices and fissures formed along with massive sunken plateaus into which water flowed. And as Genesis puts it, the waters were gathered together in one place and dry land appeared. And there was evening and morning and the third day. And God saw that it was good.

Out of that primordial, titanic struggle, water predominated two-thirds of the earth's surface and sloshed or trickled its way into every subterranean nook and cranny to make wells, springs, huge underground lakes, along with eruptive displays like Old Faithful and his cousins.

I.

Let us consider water for a moment. It is a molecule of two parts hydrogen and one part oxygen. One of the most plentiful substances on earth, it manifests itself in a variety of forms and powers.

Consider the snowflake. It really is an aggregate of tiny ice crystals formed by magnetic activity high in the atmosphere. As water vapor cools, the molecules are attracted toward one another to form the ice crystals which in turn form snowflakes. They do not come together in a haphazard manner but are formed in perfect hexagonal designs of infinite variety.

The ice crystals build themselves upon a particle of dust — dust from the earth consisting of pollen, bacteria, volcanic ash, and dust from the stars. Over 2,000 tons of stardust falls to the earth every day. On these particles the snow crystal is formed which in turn joins other crystals to make the snowflake.

Snow insulates the earth from severe cold, protecting the vulnerable seeds in the soil. A difference of temperature between the top of a snow cover and its bottom has varied as much as sixty degrees. So tiny, so delicate, so fragile is the snowflake that it can make us wishful even now for a white Christmas with sleigh bells ringing. Yet let it fall gently and constantly and it can immobilize a city like New York overnight. Of course to immobilize any city below the Mason-Dixon Line you need only about one-half inch!

But let snow collect and those trillions upon trillions of intricately designed flakes can form an avalanche that will change the face of a mountain and destroy all life in its path. So silent those snowflakes, so beautiful and intricate, yet so powerful.

Think of the power of ice. A *Titanic* is but a toy before icebergs. It can split rocks and in the form of a glacier can level hills and mountains like a behemoth bulldozer. In order to resist the power of ice at twenty degrees, a water pipe must be able to withstand a pressure of 138 tons to the square inch: "We have realized by now," says Collis in his excellent book *Vision of Glory*, "that the principalities and powers do not advertise themselves in outward splendour, they are not found in gorgeous palaces — neither spiritually, politically, nor physically" (p. 87). This power is found in tiny, humble particles of nature.

A raindrop also has power, especially when it gets together with trillions of others to form a stream or river or ocean. It corrodes and erodes the face of the earth day after day, year after year, century after century. Snow, ice, and rain have combined with wind to wear down the Rocky Mountain range. Indeed, as James Michener points out in his book *Centennial*, the Great Plains originally were in the Rockies. Water and wind have fanned the mountains into a giant plateau.

But water's greatest power is life. It is basic to every living creature, especially human beings. As we walk about we slosh a lot of water with us, perhaps as much as two-thirds of our substance. Water — and plenty of it — is vital to all life. In fact, many believe life has its origins in the primeval oceans and ponds.

Now, however, we are threatened by the massive pollution of our waters. Remember the river in New Jersey that caught fire. I have seen that river and can understand why it burned. In Minneapolis, the beautiful Mississippi winds its way in a giant gorge through the city. But a sign at river's edge near the University of Minnesota says the water is unsafe for contact with the human body. In a southern Minnesota city, a meat packing plant used to dump its blood and guts and other animal remains into a neighboring lake.

In Holland, Michigan, Lake Macatawa is slowly recovering from the massive industrial dumpings which made the lake unsafe for swimming or fishing. Lower Lake Michigan is very polluted and getting worse. For example, the pumping station which draws drinking water from the big lake used to reverse its pumps to flush its filters back into the Lake. They no longer can do that, however, because the filters get too dirty. Instead, they are constructing a special sewage treatment area to dump the crud caught in the filters. It is just too dirty to return to the lake.

Do you like lake trout or coho or whitefish? You are advised to eat no more than one a week because of the high PBB and PBC chemical content in all fish. Are you planning to fish the Chesapeake Bay? Commercial fishermen are not. Instead they are suing Allied Chemical for dumping millions of gallons of chemical waste including the exceedingly dangerous Kepone into the Bay. In Grand Rapids, Michigan, two plating companies were found to be dumping harmful chemicals into the Grand River.

Therefore we must remain vigilant in our efforts to restore and retain clean and safe water supplies. Otherwise we will not need to be on a salt sea to lament, "water, water everywhere, and not a drop to drink." We shall raise up that outcry in fresh water territory. Water's greatest power is the power to sustain life. Let us not commit racial suicide by destroying its purity.

II.

It is no surprise therefore that water should take on such importance in the world of philosophy and religion — especially religion.

Rain, for example, often was regarded as a kind of divine semen which came down to fertilize Mother Earth. Thus primitive peoples devised many rituals, dances, and rites of imitative magic to induce the gods to favor them with rain. The fertility gods and goddesses were worshiped in an effort to ensure rain and productivity of fields and flocks. If they suffered a drought, they often would do penance and offer sacrifice seeking forgiveness and gracious favor from the gods. Or they would visit the sacred prostitutes in the temples in the hope that by imitative magic, the gods might be induced to lovemaking which would ensure rain.

Water also served in rites of purification. Washings, ablutions, and baptisms abound in almost all religions. The physical nature of water is well known for its power to remove impurities. It should be no surprise that the power should transfer to the spiritual-psychological dimension. Think now of the therapeutic effect of a hot bath or shower, or a whirlpool or a soak in the mineral waters of Glenwood Springs, Colorado. These very physical experiences have a way of reaching the mind and soul.

I read somewhere that a famous actress showered many times a day. I later read about some of her immoral escapades and wondered if she, like Lady Macbeth, was trying to wash out the damned spot of guilt. Lyndon Johnson, we are told by Stuart West in his book, *Upstairs At The White House*, could not get a shower with enough pressure. Finally special pumps, pipes, and nozzles were installed that would knock over an ordinary man. Johnson surely succeeded in getting his body cleansed and massaged, but I'm not sure if it worked for his soul. When Richard Nixon moved to the

White House, he had the Johnson jet shower taken out. Some people think he should have left it in!

Some ancient peoples thought running water was the blood of the gods, and that if you were washed in it your soul could be purified. Thus water became not only a means of ablution, but of absolution. The Christian rite of baptism does not regard water the blood of the gods, of course, but it carries that symbolism of cleansing. Early Christians and many present-day ones immerse their converts in water. Others sprinkle or pour water over the candidate. Both acts symbolize the washing away of sin and the initiation into the community of Christ.

But water also stands for an inward spiritual sustenance. One of the most moving and religious of all the Psalms says:

> *O God, thou art my God, I seek thee,*
> *my soul thirsts for thee;*
> *my flesh faints for thee,*
> *as in a dry and weary land where no water is.*
> — Psalm 63:1

In another place the psalmist advises:

> *O taste and see, how gracious the Lord is.*
> *Blessed is the man that trusteth in him.*   — 34:8

The godly man is like a tree planted by streams of living water. God is seen as the water of the life of the soul.

Remember Jesus' conversation with the woman at the well? She had been seeking happiness. She had had five husbands and now was seeking for something. She had come to the well to draw water for physical life, but Jesus saw she really was seeking the water of spiritual life.

If you would have asked, I would have given you living water, he told the woman. How can that be, she replied. You have nothing with which to draw. Jesus answered, "Every one who drinks of this water (this physical water) will thirst again, but whoever drinks of the water that I shall give him will become in him a spring of water welling up to eternal life." Then with a deep pathos in her voice she said, "Sir, give me this water, that I may not thirst, nor come here to draw" (John 4:14-15).

We also go to the wells and watering places, the banquets and feasts, restaurants and dinner parties, seeking the water and bread of life. And even though we partake of the exquisite foods and liquids, we often come away from life's most sumptuous feasts with a feeling of emptiness. Something there is in the depth of our souls that is dry and thirsty. Something there is that will not be satisfied by the usual drinks.

The psalmist, realizing his soul-thirst goes on to pray:

> *So longing, I come before thee in the sanctuary*
> *to look upon thy power and glory.*
> *Thy true love is better than life;*
> *therefore I will sing thy praises.*
> *I am satisfied as with a rich and sumptuous feast*
> *and wake the echoes with thy praise.*
> — Psalm 63:2-3, 5 (NEB)

The body's thirst can be slaked by any cold drink and bring deep satisfaction that reaches almost to the soul. But not quite. The physical life can give us great joy and fulfillment, but not enough. In all our seeking and thirsting we long for another soul, someone who loves and cares, a friend whom we can trust, and an assurance that all our days are not as a tale told by an idiot, full of sound and fury, signifying nothing.

Jesus claims to be that kind of friend. If you drink from the water I give you, you will never thirst again, because it has the power to well up within you, says Jesus. It is a matter of coming to terms with yourself and God and me, says Jesus. It is a matter of recognizing that the sources of the soul's satisfactions are not in the self, nor in the physical world as such, but in God who is the source and true water of life.

If water was at the beginning, it shall also be at the end. In John's vision of heaven he hears Jesus say: "It is done: I am the Alpha and Omega, the beginning and the end. To the thirsty I will give water of life" (Revelation 21:6). Again he says, "He showed me the river of the water of life, bright as crystal, flowing from the throne of God and the Lamb through the middle of the city ..." (Revelation 22:1-2).

We have a physical thirst which must be satisfied by waters kept pure. We have a spiritual thirst which must be satisfied by spiritual waters fresh and clean. As receivers we must be cleansed by the waters of God, let ourselves be made whole and pure, regenerated and refreshed by the water of life, drinking from which, we shall never thirst again.

Prayer

Lord our God, whose majesty encompasses the most distant solar system, and before whose presence no atom goes unnoticed, we come to you in awe and wonder. Nature leads us on and on in discovery after discovery, truth after truth, insight after insight. In our thinking we are drawn into the vast areas unexplored by the mind of man. And though we have left few frontiers on the earth, we thank you for the frontiers of mind and for the assurance that all our searching is not futile. Keep us alive in thought, O God. Do not let us become lazy or cynical or conceited. Save us from the temptation to rest too comfortably in what we know. Grant us courage to proceed into the unknown, to bring it into the service of humankind and your Kingdom.

We thank you for your Spirit which pervades the world — for the power of life which impulses every plant and flower and blade of grass, for the electric souls alive with your presence, for all the pulsations which stimulate the world to vibrant ecstasy.

We ask for a greater gift of your Spirit. Look with pity upon those of us who are withdrawn and beaten. Observe with gracious favor the empty and despairing, the famished and forsaken. In a time of spiritual sickness in nation and Church, be gracious to us once again, good Lord. Lead us to honesty and humility. Take away the arrogance and pride which close us to your presence. Save us from presumption and preoccupation with our own scheme for things. Help us to be open to you, that our souls might be refreshed and refined for a life meaningful and free. Take away the allurements of false waters of life, which become brackish with time and bitter in the heart.

Come to us with your aid for our individual needs — for help in our relationships, for struggles in our identity — we want to know who we are and who you want us to be. Lead us to a new understanding. Through Jesus Christ our Lord. Amen.

19. Thirst — And The Living Waters

Jesus said to her, "Every one who drinks of this water will thirst again, but whoever drinks of the water that I shall give him will never thirst; the water that I shall give him will become in him a spring of water welling up to eternal life."
— John 4:13-14

It may come as a great reminder to note that we human beings are largely composed of water. The orange juice and coffee we drank this morning were mostly water. The eggs and toast, jellies and jams we enjoyed were a higher percentage of water than we realized. The vegetables and fruits we eat are a high percentage of water.

And even the air we are breathing has a high moisture content, sometimes as we well know on summer days, as high as 100 percent humidity. Thus, if the truth be known, and if we could really see ourselves with the exceptional eye, we would see we are essentially water sloshing about in these mysteriously organized cells and organs and bones. Take away our bodily water and the residue would be rather small indeed.

Much the same can be said for the earth. About seventy percent of the earth's surface is covered by water. If Mount Everest is a little over 29,000 feet above the earth, the Marianas Trench of the ocean goes down 35,600 feet below sea level. The average depth of the ocean, says Marsten Bates of the University of Michigan, is about 12,500 feet, whereas the average elevation of our continents is 2,500 feet. In other words, if our earth had a smooth surface, the water of the sea "would cover it to a uniform depth of about a mile and a half," says Dr. Bates (*The Forest and the Sea*, p. 43).

Seawater is a kind of magical substance, says Bates. You can't make it up in the laboratory by putting all the proper chemicals together. It has a mystical, life-giving, life-supporting quality about it — a quality that seems to have remained more or less the same for two billion years. Life exists in microscopic to behemoth sizes in the ocean. And even the whales depend upon the tiny plankton for their survival.

In a marine laboratory in England, it was discovered that one cubic foot of seawater contains at the very least twelve and a half million plant cells! Thus, when our children scoop a bucket of the ocean in their beach buckets they are literally carrying a microscopic universe in their hands. Is it any wonder L. J. Henderson has observed that, "No philosopher's or poet's fancy, no myth of a primitive people has ever exaggerated the importance, the usefulness, and above all the marvelous beneficence of the ocean for the community of living things" (*The Fitness of the Environment*, quoted in Bates, p. 43).

But much can be said for the fresh waters of the world. The Mississippi River empties into the Gulf of Mexico every minute of every day forty acres of water, twenty feet deep. The Amazon exceeds that by dumping one hundred acres of water every minute into its mouth. Add to that the Nile, the Yellow, the Danube, the Rhine, the Volga, the Thames, and hundreds more rivers, and we see the vast, moving waters of the earth — powerful, churning, flushing the earth into the sea. And the sea in turn, with the sun as a gigantic furnace, evaporates the seawater, leaving the salt behind and returns it to the earth in the form of rain. Yes, rain, by the tons in tiny drops, carefully dispersed so as not to destroy the most delicate of flowers. Yes, rain, which over the millions of years has chiseled the earth's rock into soil for all the world's bread and wine.

But concentrate then on the single forest pond, as did Franklin Russell for a year through the four seasons. A pond is a microcosm of the world, a biosphere unto itself, providing life to insects and worms and fish beyond number. For example, Russell determined that about five hundred million earthworms received the water of life from around the banks of that small pond. "A pinch of pond soil," says Russell, "may enfold a million of the simplest animals on earth and scores of the simplest plants and millions of funguses and bacteria" (Russell, *Watchers at the Pond*, pp.12-13). So, mothers, your child is getting more nutrients from that mud in his mouth than you realize!

And should there be a willow tree at pond's edge, it will lift water up its trunk 150 feet in an hour, and in summer can heave a ton of water everyday, making as many as six million leaves a season on a single elm. Water, water, it's everywhere, and most of it is to drink as the water of life for all living things. Water, water, everywhere, composed of two parts of volatile hydrogen with one part of volatile oxygen to cover seventy percent of the earth's surface and to constitute a significant percentage of our body.

I.

Are you thirsty? Would you like a cold, refreshing sip of water from a bubbling spring in Maine? Is there anything better on a hot summer afternoon after gardening than a tall glass of sparkling ice water?

Jesus knew the feeling. He and his disciples were traveling north again, back to his native Galilee from the south, from Judea. Prudence would have had them take the friendlier eastern route through Perea, but they chose instead the shorter, potentially hostile, route through Samaria.

The Jews and the Samaritans had been at odds for years. When the Assyrians conquered Israel in 722 B.C., they colonized it with foreigners, with Gentiles who eventually intermarried with the Jews. When Ezra and Nehemiah proposed their reforms after the Babylonian Exile in the late sixth century B.C., they urged divorce from Gentile wives. Samaritans not only refused, they claimed to be the true Israel and built a Temple on Mount Gerizim to rival the one on Mount Zion in Jerusalem.

Thus, Jesus and his Jewish disciples were at some risk traveling through Samaria. Tired and hot at midday, Jesus sat down to rest at the ancient well of Jacob, while his disciples went off to buy food, of all places in a non-kosher Samaritan village! That is when this intriguing and richly instructive conversation between Jesus and the Samaritan woman takes place.

There are several strange things happening. One is that Jesus the Jew is in Samaritan territory. Another is that he is not only talking with a despised Samaritan, but with of all things, a Samaritan woman! He is breaking a number of the cultural taboos of the time.

Further, thirsty as he was, he asked her for a drink from the well. No doubt her bucket or leather skin and ropes used to draw water from the 100-foot deep well were ritually unclean. Further, she was an "unclean" woman herself, not only because she was a Samaritan, but because she was five times married and divorced and now living with another man.

She was ostracized by the other women of the village. That is why she was at this well, a half mile from the village, and at noon, rather than morning or evening when the other women came together to draw water — and to gossip — no doubt about her.

Jesus broke down the religious, geographic, historic, and cultural barriers by asking her for a drink from the ancient well. Jesus himself had need of water — cool, clear, physical water, two parts hydrogen and one part oxygen. John's Gospel presents no Gnostic deity, no fleshless divinity when he presents Jesus as the Son of God.

Contradicting the ever-popular dualism of the time, John insists the Word of God, the Logos or Reason of God, became flesh and dwelt among us. He ate as we eat. He experienced pain as we experience pain. He became weary and thirsty as we become weary and thirsty. So he asked of the non-kosher, unacceptable woman, an outsider not only to Jews, but to her fellow Samaritan women, he asked of her, "Give me a drink."

Thus here, as always, Jesus affirms the goodness and necessity of the physical body and world. Here, as always, he embraces the necessity of physical water as he did of the necessity and delight of physical food and wine at the many banquets and dinner parties he attended.

So for Jesus, true religion is not a denial of our real humanity, our real hunger and thirst, our real taste for water and all the beverages which boast it as their principle component. We are thirsty and the Son of God slakes his thirst at even the hands of an outsider and enemy.

II.

But, as usual, Jesus took the issue to a deeper level. He first asks the woman to give to him a drink. He then reverses roles and says if she would ask him, he would give her living water, which if she drank she would never thirst again.

And her response indicates she didn't quite get it at first. She requests that water so she can be free of the drudgery of drawing and carrying water from the well the long distance home. But Jesus had in mind a deeper kind of water, a living water, a spiritual nurturant which satisfies the thirst of the soul and slakes the heart with the soothing reassurance of eternal life.

Let's look at the woman again. One thing a conversation with Jesus produces is honesty — honesty about one's situation and one's self. Perhaps it is Jesus' approachable manner, his accepting, non-condemnatory demeanor, which elicits confession and truthfulness in us all. Most all of us know, we cannot be in the presence of the living Christ very long without coming clean about ourselves, without coming to the truth, without facing up to the real situation.

And what was the real situation with the Samaritan woman? The real situation is this: she is famished in heart and soul. She is hungry and thirsty for a deeper, inward satisfaction she has not been able to find in her five husbands and now in her lover.

The truth is the Samaritan woman was like many of us today who believe the answer to our inward longing is to be found only in good food and wine and sensual pleasure. I remember reading about a man in England who bragged he had made love to 2,000 women in his effort to find love. "Did you find it?" the newspaper reporter asked. "No, I have not found true love," said the Englishman who made Don Juan look like a monk.

"Have you found true love?" Jesus was in effect asking the Samaritan woman. And she in effect answered she hadn't, but wanted it. We are like her, many of us, who affirm only the materialistic, sensuous side of life. We assume we can slake the soul's thirst with the world's finest wines and fill our hearts with the world's gourmet foods. We seem to think true love will arrive with yet another affair and yet another sensuous high.

We need all that of course — food and wine and the sensuous experience. Jesus affirmed that when he said, "Give me a drink from Jacob's well." But he said and always says, "If you ask me I will give a drink of spiritual water which will well up into eternal life, and from which drinking you will never thirst again."

And I have to tell you that as much as I love the waters of the world, the seas, the rivers and lakes, the rainstorms and ponds, and all the watered drink and foods for the body; it is the water of the soul which satisfies eternally — the water of the soul and heart and mind, the water of the Living Word which stimulates, challenges, and energizes, the water which cleanses the soul and fortifies the spirit; the water which penetrates the deepest reaches of our parched egos and lonely hearts and infuses them with a life which says you are accepted, you are forgiven, you are affirmed, you are loved.

What spouses and lovers, vintners and gourmet chefs cannot do for us, the Living Word of God can. For centuries the Word has organized creation and stimulated us in awe and wonder before the miraculous waters of the world.

But even more, the Word of God, the Logos, the rational ordering, structuring principle of the universe, manifested in the Christ, has slaked the soul with living water. Whether it is the Bible itself, or the ancient Gregorian chant, or Mozart's *Requiem*, or Beethoven's *Ninth*, or Strauss' *Death and Transfiguration*, or Michelangelo's *David*, or Blake's poetry, or Handel's *Messiah*, this living water keeps on slaking our soul-thirst in a thousand concert halls, in thousands of libraries and universities and museums, in hundreds of thousands of churches and on the very cutting edges of all knowledge and exploration and discovery.

O Lord, give us this water, this living, eternal, life-giving water always. And he does, because at the end he says, "I am the Alpha and Omega, the beginning and end. To the thirsty I will give water without price from the fountain of the water of life" (Revelation 21:6). And that, dear friends, is the gospel, the good news.

Prayer

O Eternal God, by whose good pleasure all the galaxies and solar systems have been thrown into place, and by whose creative power the seed of life has been sown in the earth, with all its mystery and complexity, we praise and adore you for the fecundity of all living things and for your providential care for us in food and drink.

O God, whose pleasure it was to brood upon the primeval waters of the world, and then to separate sea and dry land and to set in place rivers and lakes and the fountains of the deep, we praise you for the gift of water — for cool streams and bubbling springs, for salt seas and fresh lakes, for the early morning shower and the soothing, late evening bath. From the miraculous birth waters of the womb, to the last cup of cold water given in your name at our death, you sustain us with your life-giving water.

We confess our terrible misuse of water. Even now in time of storm, we dump our raw sewage into it. We pollute it with chemicals and waste, so much so that even our fire-quenching water has itself caught fire. Awaken political and business and other leaders, and arouse us all to a higher resolve to purify and cleanse our waters — these waters of life.

If in summer heat our bodies thirst for refreshment, in all seasons of life our hearts and souls and minds thirst after you, O God, ever-flowing fountain of life for all living things. We confess that in our soul-thirst we often remain in stagnant pools of thought, or become content with the stale waters of routine and comfort. Having once been refreshed and enlightened, we tend to close off ourselves to new refreshment and enlightenment. Forgive us, O God, and help us to be open to your ever-flowing stream of knowledge and truth.

We pray for help to clean up the information streams of our society. Help us to resist those who would entice us and fill our minds with sludge for the sake of profit. Cause us to resist the dogmatist who suppresses truth and the traditionalist who would stifle it.

Even now, in this very hour, give us a drink from the deep wells of your eternal truth, O God. If we are lonely, if we are mourning, if we are sorely tempted, if we are without work or true friends, if we are famished in soul, discouraged and even depressed; come to us, O Living Stream of all Life, and refresh us that we shall be strong and radiant, newly energized and so resolved to serve your Cause. Through Jesus Christ our Lord. Amen.

20. Dinner With A Jealous Brother

He answered his father, "Lo, these many years I have served you, and I never disobeyed your command; yet you never gave me a kid, that I might make merry with my friends." — Luke 15:29

It was a classic scene right out of the heart of Protestant evangelicalism. Reminiscent of the revivalism of the nineteenth century, and bordering on the Pentecostalism of the twentieth century, the scene evokes both repugnance and nostalgia — repugnance for a mode of religion, which seems hypocritical and out of fashion; but nostalgia for a religion which genuinely affects the spirit and provokes a change of heart.

It was a summer Sunday morning in the South. The hymn singing had been especially enthusiastic. The extemporaneous prayers had been earnest and heartfelt. And now it was testimony time — time for people to stand up and speak publicly about the way the Lord had come to them to change their lives. It was the occasion to say publicly how bad they had been, and then to say even more publicly and enthusiastically how they had been saved. "Once I was lost, but now I am found," the testifier would say in front of the whole congregation.

One man had recently come into the church and had genuinely experienced conversion and transformation. Known around town as an intriguing, interesting, but a slightly roguish man, his conversion had made the ecclesiastical headlines. It was not "Guess who's coming to dinner?" but, "Guess who's coming to church?" Yes, he really is. Who would have believed it?

So when, on that bright and warm Sunday morning, the dapper, dashing man about town went up to the microphone to testify about what the Lord had done for him, the whole church was attentive. For as we could say, paraphrasing the old television commercial about a brokerage house, "When a repentant sinner speaks, everyone listens."

And listen they did. They were on the edge of their seats as step by step he recounted the waywardness of his former life. There was party after party with gourmet food, too much booze, and abundant vintage wine. Racy, provocative movies were shown in the company of equally racy, provocative women.

But it didn't stop there. He told of his times in Vegas at the gambling tables, losing some, yes, but winning big too. And then there were the riverboat cruises on the mighty Mississippi, with wine, women, and song, and of course, the casino, where he had his share of excitement.

It was a fast crowd of jet setters in a modest sort of way — parties, booze, girls, gambling. He had it all. And then there were the drugs — marijuana, at first, and then heroine and cocaine. They were high, touching the clouds. And the girls were there in abundance.

As he spoke, the summer Sunday morning crowd sat forward on the edge of the pews, straining to hear every word. Mothers were embarrassed for their children, but too intrigued to take them out for fear of missing something. Fathers shuffled their feet and nodded knowingly, inwardly. It was so still and quiet you could hear the drop of the proverbial pin. People hardly dared to breathe for fear of missing a juicy detail.

And then the dashing, dapper, one-time intriguing rogue said he felt it was time to give up his sinful ways, and to give his life to the Lord instead of wasting it with the Devil. And now, thank God, he had experienced grace and had been saved.

With that announcement, the congregation settled back in their seats. The children were sent out to Sunday school, the men coughed their long-repressed coughs, the women found their Kleenexes in their purses, the teenagers yawned, and the general rustle and bustle of a steaming congregation resumed as the converted sinner attempted to relate the beauties of the new life he had found. But sensing he had lost his audience, he praised the Lord, and sat down to a few weak amens.

I.

So it was with the younger son in the world's most famous and classic short story — the story of the prodigal son. Sin seems always so much more interesting than salvation, and the wayward life seems always more intriguing than the good life. The life of passion seems far more alluring than the life of sweet reasonableness. And gray rationality fades in the presence of the flowing reds of lust and desire.

We hold our breath, sit on the edge of the seat, and listen for any suggested sin or pleasure we haven't tried when we listen to this story. As Mae West once said, "When I have to choose between two evils, I always like to choose the one I haven't tried!"

There's a lot to be said for the younger son even if he does get all the best press in this story. He gets the best press because so many of us identify with him and his escapades, or think we might *like* to identify with him and his escapades.

Whatever else you can say about the younger son, he was not stodgy. Nor was he fearful. Reckless, maybe, but not fearful. He was willing to launch out, to take risks, to venture away from the securities of family and home, to experiment with the far country. He was a risk taker.

He represents the type who is willing to leave the securities of the corporation to start a business of his own. He symbolizes the woman who is willing to break out of an irreparable, abusive marriage to attempt a new life for herself. This prodigal — innocent, inexperienced, and naïve though he may be — is not a coward. He is willing to take chances, to see what's on the other side of the mountain or country or world.

If there is a bit of the repressed rascal and rogue in all of us, there is also in many of us the repressed writer or artist or inventor or adventurer. Confined in the comfort of routine and content in the security of blue chip investments, there remains in many of us the vague feeling we may have missed something important, something crucial and exciting. This younger son intrigues us because he did what we sometimes dreamed of doing — going to the "far country" — the far country of non-conformity and counterculturism and to the life of freedom.

Goodness and God seem so often boring. Any movie or television show or novel doesn't know how to portray goodness in an interesting way. I am reminded of one of my favorite *New Yorker* cartoons, which depicts two men conversing in heaven. They are standing on a cloud, before a wall which has cracked plaster with smudges and stains. Their once-white robes are torn, patched, and soiled. Their halos are bent and tarnished. Picking their teeth, one man says to the other, "I don't know about you, but I always thought it would be better than this!"

Boring as the good life is portrayed to be, the life of recklessness and selfishness and waywardness often comes to a disastrous end. The far country of desire often ends up in unwanted pregnancies and abortions, sexually-transmitted diseases, and the violence of deep emotions betrayed. The far country of passion often leads from anger to rage to murder or suicide. The far country of the perpetual good life often has addiction or bankruptcy or a fried brain as its destination.

But strangely enough, the "far country" where one is totally lost can become the place where one is totally found, or the place where one finds himself or comes to himself. Very often one needs the "far country" where we are stripped of the security of family and reputation and money to come to terms with our own frailty, our own weakness, our own temporality and brevity of days upon the earth — to come to terms with our own death.

That is the beauty of the younger son and the far country. For it was there he came to himself and said, "I will return to my father." Rogues and rascals we may be, repressed or otherwise, but many of us identify with that younger son. Because at the very end of all our non-conformity and risk taking and creativity and riotous living — underneath it all we hope we "come to ourselves" to return to our Father.

II.

When we come to the older brother in this, the world's most perfect short story, most of us are like the congregation listening to the repentant sinner now talking about his new religious life. We were much more intrigued with his sin than his salvation, and we were much more fascinated with his wild adventures than with his settled life in his heavenly home.

So too with this poor elder brother who always gets a bad rap in this story. No one wants to be like the older brother — at least openly, but probably in actuality, more of us are like the older brother than we like to admit.

If the younger brother is a number two type son, the older brother is a number one type son. He always obeyed his parents, came home from the date on time, made his bed, picked up his clothes, cleaned up both his room and his plate. He always colored *within* the lines, never put a dent in the car, and did *what* he was told *when* he was told.

The number two type son never colors within the lines, leaves his room, his clothes, and the car a mess. He misses appointments, flaunts commitments, is usually late, gets bad grades, and exasperates his parents. He exasperates his parents because he has figured out that is the only way to get attention. After all, his parents have shelves of photograph albums of his older brother when *he* was young, but only one-third an album of photos of his infancy and childhood. His brother's baby album is complete with detailed history of first words and first steps and is adorned with locks of hair and baby teeth. The younger brother's baby book is only partially filled and has never been found.

But let us say a good word for the older brother, number one type sons. In the parable they probably represent the scribes and Pharisees, the rule-keeping, somewhat rigid religious leaders of the time. Conservative stay-at-homes they may have been, but they were the ones that copied the Sacred Scriptures by hand for centuries so number two type sons could continue to read them. And the number two types could read them only because the number one type scholars and teachers patiently and painstakingly taught them how to read and write.

So in our time if the Baby Boomers and Generation X-ers are anti-institutional religion, picking and choosing their spirituality wherever they can buy it in the spirituality consumers' marketplace — if they are that, the number one type institutional churches continue day after day, week after week, year after year to teach the

Sacred Scriptures and traditions, so that when the wanderers come home, the churches have to take them in as in Robert Frost's return of the hired man.

And come to think of it, when the number two types do decide to go to the far country to seek their fortune and perchance to find themselves, they often take a plane or train run by the dutiful hardworking stay at home, wish-we-could-go-with-you number one types. If the number two type hippies and flower children of the '60s and '70s led the needed countercultural revolution, the number one types of the '40s and '50s generation financed them.

The number one types are often the accountants, the bookkeepers, the controllers, the Chief Financial Officers. They are the judges, the policemen, the law and order devotees, the control freaks. They tend to be most happy when things are scheduled, reported, accounted for, inventoried, cleaned, organized, in step, and in line. So we desperately need them in the post office, in the backrooms of financial firms and in air controller towers. The number one types usually are incurably legalistic, but at least we can credit them for keeping the law.

If number two types cannot always be counted on, number one types are devoted to duty. They will make a product and get it to you on time. The rest of the world may be partying, but they will be devoted to duty. You can count on them. They will not be loafing or goofing off. They will be at work, thank God, servicing their mortgages and car payments and credit card debt like the rest of us.

To tell you the truth, without the number one types, the world would come to a grinding halt. So at bottom, we really need this older brother of Jesus' famous story. So why does he come off as the bad guy?

III.

For insight we now turn to the father. And one of the big questions for the father is whether he can get his two sons, these jealous brothers, to sit down to dinner together to reconcile. Because the truth is they both are jealous and resentful.

The resentful older brother is not about to come into a big party to celebrate the return of his wastrel brother. After all, the older brother had been working hard all of these years while the number two type was out spending extravagantly, having a great time with wine, women, and song. More than that, after the younger brother had taken his one-third of the estate, the older brother had to work just that much harder to build it up again.

But there was another resentment and jealousy. If the truth be known, the older brother was jealous that he did not know *how* to have a good time. He did not know how to "let go," to "let his hair down," to relax and laugh and enjoy. So dutiful and so anxious to please, he was deeply fearful he would be rejected if people knew his total self which also longed for freedom and risk. Inwardly, he longed for a release from his stultified role of always having to do things right, to be good and to bear all the responsibility. But he feared to step outside the role lest he lose the approval he so much needed for his self-esteem.

More than that, when the father wants to throw the big welcome home party for the younger brother, it seems as though he is rewarding sin and waste and profligacy. He should have made the boy come crawling on his knees begging for forgiveness, fed him on penitential bread and water, and put him on probation for five years. But no, instead this party, this fatted calf, the best robe, and ring and shoes. How can this be?

It can be because it is the father's good nature to be gracious and forgiving — both to number one types and to number two types. It can be because the father's banquet was not intended to reward profligacy, but to celebrate repentance and change of heart and filial love. The banquet was a celebration of resurrection, for your brother who was lost is now found. He who was dead is now alive. In that sense, the Father's eyes are ever toward the far country, looking down the road for sons and daughters bound for home so he can give them a grand welcome home resurrection banquet.

But there's another jealousy involved, and another resentment too. It is that of the younger brother who knows that, unlike his brother who wisely and faithfully kept the business going during his absence — unlike him, in the name of freedom and creativity, he did not find fame and fortune — he blew them.

And he is resentful of the fact that even though he did "find himself" he still is broke and will now have to work for his brother once his father is gone. The very oppressiveness of the older brother he tried to escape now threatens once again to close in on him.

But the father goes out to both sons — out to greet the one returning from waywardness and profligacy, out to greet the other wanting to return from the burden of all work and no play and from the odiousness of always having to be right and good so as to be accepted. The beauty of this story is that the father's love is stronger than either son's deep sense of unworthiness.

And God is the Father. And he bids all us younger and older brother types, all us number one types and number two types, to put aside fears of unworthiness, to confess them, and to sit down together in the great welcome home banquet planned for us. You are accepted and celebrated. I am accepted and celebrated.

And you and the folks in that southern summer church will be surprised, as will the fellows in the *New Yorker*'s tacky heaven. The resurrection banquet is far more exciting than we ever imagined — jealous brothers and sisters will sit down to dine together in God's great feast of mercy and grace. So put them aside now — the jealousies, the resentments, the self-righteousness as well as the self-loathing, and come to the party. You are loved. You are accepted.

Prayer

Almighty God, Father of our Lord Jesus Christ and our Father, who has designed us for families and communities and nations, and who seeks to "find yourself" in relationship with us as we seek to "find ourselves" in relationship with you and others, we praise and adore you for the gift of life and the mystery of loving personalities.

In your holy and fatherly presence, we are conscious of our feeble efforts at effective fathering and mothering. You are all-powerful and yet all-patient, whereas we so often feel powerless and exhibit great impatience. Yourself, the very essence of goodness, you nonetheless readily forgive our wrongs amid waywardness. Ourselves, so often neglectful of right thinking and acting, harbor grudges and wait for the opportunity for revenge. Be pleased to forgive us, O God, and aid us in our parenting and grand parenting.

O God, who has designed us for families and for the enrichment which comes from brothers and sisters, we bring before you the agonies of our persistent sibling rivalries. Some of us have been oppressive and obnoxious with our siblings. Some of us have been distant and uncaring. Others of us have been hostile and vengeful. O Heavenly Father, who has intended our earthly family life to be a taste of your heavenly family, grant us grace to forgive and strength to reconcile with our brothers and sisters, our stepbrothers and stepsisters. Help us to know the deep joy of genuine sharing and mutual support.

And grant us all, O Lord, an extended family of spiritual kinfolk, people committed to you and your way. Bind all the family of humankind together in renewed commitment to justice and peace. Through Jesus Christ our Lord. Amen.

21. Communion And Companionship

Because there is one bread, we who are many are one body, for we all partake of one bread.
— 1 Corinthians 10:17

Those of us raised in the Protestant and Reformed traditions often have forgotten that historic religions frequently are centered around feasts and feast days. Ancient Judaism, for example, abounded with feasts, as did the mystery religions and fertility cults of Egypt, Greece, and Rome. Both Western and Eastern Christianity have continued many aspects of the sacred feast, where the religious devotees eat and drink together as one people in the presence of God.

The sparse, spartan, unadorned nature of Protestantism was vividly portrayed in the beautiful contrasts in the movie, *Babette's Feast*. The setting is on a remote coast of Jutland, where a Protestant minister has established a strict, world-denying, otherworldly sect. Grey, somber, and eschewing the pleasures of the present life, they live a life of simplicity and barrenness, devoid of the art and glory of the present world — a world regarded more or less as evil.

The stark self-denial is no more apparent than in the food which consists of dried fish and hard stale bread, served day after day in ritual monotony. After the minister's death, his two lovely daughters carry on his work amidst an increasingly quarrelsome and fractious congregation. Babette, a refugee from the French Revolution, then comes to be cook and housekeeper for the two sisters. By good fortune, she wins 10,000 francs in the French lottery. Out of her love and grace, she asks the sisters if she might prepare a truly French feast for the religious group to enjoy.

As a former chef in a famous Paris restaurant, Babette has mastered the art of finest French cuisine. The elaborate purchases and preparations have been made. But feeling guilty over the approaching excesses of food and wine, the sisters confess their faults to the community. They agree to come to the feast, but to act as though they could not taste the exquisite wine and food.

While words would not express appreciation for the culinary masterpiece they were enjoying, eyes and subtle facial expressions betrayed the depth of their satisfaction. Beautifully and strangely, as the exquisite feast continued, old hostilities were laid aside. Confessions were made and forgiveness granted. And at the close, the community joined hands in a circle of love heretofore impossible.

Beautifully and wonderfully, it was Babette's feast which became a true Lord's Supper, a sacrament of grace, where, in the breaking of bread and sharing of wine, true communication and companionship were restored. The stoic barrenness of the northern, reserved Protestants was released into a life-affirming, brother-sister embracing banquet of bounty and blessing. It was at the common table, sharing the common bread and wine, that true communion and companionship were restored. And they came to experience that of which Conrad Aiken later wrote: "Music I heard with you was more than music, And bread I broke with you was more than bread...." Communion and companionship go together and speak of more than we know.

I.

Consider first *companionship*.

The word "companion" comes from two words which mean "to share bread together." Thus a company is literally a group which shares bread, an idea which takes on special meaning when we think of "bread" in the colloquial sense as money. In the Bible's world of the ancient Near East, to break bread together, to share a meal together, was a special act of fellowship and sharing. Hostilities and enmities were to be left outside as one went in to eat with another.

When Paul wrote to the Corinthian Christians in Corinth, Greece, he was addressing the important question of companionship. Common to the ancient world, Corinth had temples devoted to the ancient gods. People offered animal sacrifices and breads to the gods. After the sacrifice the meat would be butchered and a religious feast would be eaten in the presence of the deity.

The question for Corinthian Christians was this: Should they any longer eat at these religious banquets held in honor of pagan deities? In brief, the answer was no. Because in ancient thinking, to eat and drink the dedicated foods was to be joined in companionship with the god to whom they were dedicated. Since those gods were idols, Christians should not be linked with them. To break bread with them was to have companionship with the false gods. Instead, they were to break bread at Christ's table to have companionship with him, and to be controlled by his mind, his ideas.

Likewise he might advise married people and families today. In her autobiography, *Two-Part Invention*, which recounts her marriage and her husband's death from cancer, Madeline L'Engle speaks of the sacrament of the common meal. She loved to cook and recalls how their best times together were before the fire in the evening with a drink and then enjoying a fine dinner together. It was in the breaking of bread, in the sharing of good wine and food (some of which they had grown themselves), that their love and understanding deepened.

Paul knew that if the Corinthian Christians ate at the pagan feasts they might come under the power of the prevailing ideas of the pagan religion. It was better they gather in communion and companionship around the Lord's Table so as to be influenced predominantly by his ideas.

So too Christians and families today. Regrettably, many couples and families eat on the run. Our homes come to look more like motels and fast-food restaurants where we grab a few winks and a few bites before we are off to our next activity. We rightly ask, when is it families truly break bread together to sense they are a company, made special by prevailing ideas significantly shared? Perhaps some of our inherent loneliness and alienation is due to the fact that our common meals have become less a sacrament of grace than "meals on wheels." We can say much the same for the Lord's Supper or Communion. Regrettably many Protestants have displaced the Communion from centrality and frequency in worship. Typically, in many Protestant Churches, attendance drops, rather than rises, on Communion Sundays.

But when we gather around the Communion table to break bread and drink wine, we give Christ opportunity to influence us with his prevailing ideas. Gathered at that table, we are reminded of our common humanity dependent not only on physical bread and wine, but on the spiritual bread and wine by which our souls are fed. Couples and families who gather for Communion experience a bonding that is both physical and spiritual, and are strengthened in their love for one another, as is the Church.

As Aiken put it: "Music I heard with you was more than music, And bread I broke with you was more than bread...."

II.

When we speak of companionship we are almost immediately speaking of *communication*. Sharing bread and wine together almost inevitably leads to communication.

Some years ago while traveling through Europe, my wife and I stopped in Germany at a restaurant on the Autobahn for lunch. There were only two places left at an outdoor table for four. The other two places were occupied by two older German gentlemen. We were invited to join them.

As we proceeded with lunch we made efforts at communication. My wife Sara and I knew about five words in German and they knew about five in English. Despite that, through words and gestures we learned about them and they about us. Even more significant, they may well have fought in World War II against our relatives and family friends. But a few years later we were breaking bread together in a country which once had been the scene of terrible bloodshed. Breaking bread together and communicating. Would to God that could have happened to prevent World War II.

But breaking bread and communicating can help prevent personal and family atrocities. Over the years, couples have told me how easy it is to get caught in a routine where they never have time to communicate. Younger families are caught up in work, school and athletic schedules, community organizations, and church. By the time the children are in bed, couples are too tired to talk.

At a couple's retreat discussing that very problem, the group suggested changing the routine. Go out to lunch together. And they did. Some even went out to breakfast together or to brunch on weekends. They did it even though Winston Churchill once remarked that the secret to a long and happy marriage was never to have breakfast with your spouse! Madeline L'Engle agrees!

Breakfast or no breakfast, couples and families need time to communicate. And well-prepared, leisurely meals can be the occasions not only of talking about ideas or happenings, but occasions of sharing feelings and dreams within the context of love and acceptance. Companionship and communication make us feel more loved, more complete, more human, more in touch with everything that is important.

Older couples may have the opposite problem. A *New Yorker* cartoon has a woman telling her friend, "He knows what I'm going to say, and I know what he's going to say, so we never say anything!" Indeed.

They are like the couple who at their fiftieth wedding anniversary party were sitting at the head table. The husband leaned over to his hard-of-hearing wife and said, "Honey, I'm proud of you." "What?" she said. "Honey, I'm proud of you!" he repeated. She replied, "That's okay. I'm tired of you too!"

Couples and Christians like that need the incursion of new realities and new ideas within their lives. They need the zest for life a 92-year-old friend of mine had. His library was full of books he had read and new books and magazines he was in the process of reading. Married over sixty years, he daily gave his wife a new compliment. Couples today need what my friend had. They need new books and experiences, new music and new art. Perhaps most of all they need new religion — a religion that keeps us alive with faith, hope, and love for the future God has in mind for us.

So it is as Christian couples and families and singles we come around the Communion table for companionship, for breaking bread and sharing wine, to increase our love for God and for one another. Putting aside the all-too-familiar barrenness and dualism of Protestantism, we should gather for "Babette's Feast," a banquet of God's grace and graciousness.

May God bless all our families and friendships and our Church, and the Church universal, with true communication and communion. Then may we say with Aiken: "Music I heard with you was more than music, And bread I broke with you was more than bread...."

Prayer

Eternal God, creative energy of the universe who has manifested yourself in power, and who has ordained our solar system to have its center and source in the light of the sun, we praise you for the light-energy which empowers every living creature upon the earth. Because of sunshine we have rain, and together they give us bountiful fields and vineyards, and faces radiant with the glow of life. Our bodies live because of your light and life, O Lord. We give you thanks and praise.

As you have given us food for the body, so too have you nourished our minds and souls with your words of truth and love, life and grace. Through lawgivers and prophets, through teachers and apostles, and uniquely through your Son, Jesus Christ, you have provided the Word above all words. We give thanks for Jesus, for the grace and truth fully manifested in him.

Grant to us today, O Lord, the nourishment we need for body and soul. For those without bread in the world, we pray a new generosity and a world economy to enable all to eat well. But for those of us well-fed in body who have forgotten we cannot live by bread alone, grant a new openness really to hear the words which proceed from your mouth of wisdom and truth. Save us from illusion, from deceitfulness and hypocrisy, from falsification and fabrication.

Release us from our hunger for the salacious and our thirst for violence. Feed us on your words of kindness, thoughtfulness, justice, fairness, patience, mercy, and understanding. Cause our souls to grow beyond spiritual infancy, whining only for the pabulum of your word, when we should be craving the meat of your truth for mature Christian living.

Forgive us then our lack of study of the Bible and our neglect of the Church's historic reservoir of wisdom. Save us from obsession with whimsical, trendy thinking so that we might center our lives more fully upon your substantial and abiding truths. So bring us at last to the fullness of the stature of Christ, we pray. Amen.

22. Chicken Soup And Other Remedies

> *Finally, brethren, whatever is true, whatever is honorable, whatever is just, whatever is pure, whatever is lovely, whatever is gracious, if there is any excellence, if there is anything worthy of praise, think about these things.*
> — Philippians 4:8

It was one of those memorable Sunday mornings in church. It was fall, in November. The air was crisp and dry. The leaves were gone except for a straggler here and there, and the bare branches were silhouetted against a crystalline blue sky. It was one of those Sunday mornings, peaceful and serene, when we celebrate our living and want to say, "God's in his heaven and all is right with the world."

And it seemed just as beautiful inside the church as it was outside. Our Sunday morning seminar, meeting between the services, was packed to overflowing. In our effort to broaden our understanding of contemporary Judaism, we had invited a guest speaker, a popular rabbi from one of the neighboring synagogues.

The rabbi gave us a brief historical backdrop and then surveyed contemporary Judaism with consummate skill and finesse. It had been a very satisfying historical and theological feast, and then came time for questions from the floor.

In the back of the room an older lady raised her hand. As she stood to speak, I wondered what theologically profound question she might have for the rabbi. "Rabbi," she said, "I wonder if you could tell me why it is that so many Jewish mothers I know believe so strongly in the medicinal powers of chicken soup!" The whole seminar crowd rolled with laughter, as did the rabbi and I.

"Well," said the rabbi, "it is true that a lot of Jewish mothers believe in the medicinal powers of chicken soup. And there probably are some therapeutic powers in chicken soup." He paused a moment, and then continued, "However, if other Jewish mothers were anything like my mother, the medicinal power was not so much in the soup itself as in the love with which it was given." The group applauded.

How was it with your mother? My mother was not Jewish, but she, like many Jewish mothers, seemed to equate food with love. She grew many of her own vegetables and regularly treated her family to tasty, fresh, American cuisine. Anyone who ever ate one of her big, red, tender, juicy tomatoes would understand why a tomato is not a vegetable, but a fruit.

For her, food was love and love was food. Meals were family occasions around the kitchen or dining room table. Let no child come to the table with dirty hands, uncombed hair, or slovenly appearance. Food was love and love was food. Meals were sacramental times, times for saying grace, sharing the happenings of the day, telling jokes, and of course, helping with the dishes. Yes, chicken soup was sometimes a part of it, but it was all food, not only for the body, but for the soul — a fact I took for granted until I grew older.

If we need chicken soup for an aching, feverish body, we also need chicken soup for an aching, feverish soul. How often in my many years in the ministry I have wished I could say to people in distress, "Here, take these pills every four hours and eat a big bowl of chicken soup every day and you will be better."

Regrettably, when it comes to the mind and soul, when it comes to the heart and spirit, when it comes to our inmost being, it is not quite that easy. Yet, there are remedies for soul sickness. Thank God, there are powerful remedies for those things which perplex and vex us, for those things which nag at us most deeply, even, thank God, remedies for the soul-sickness unto death.

And many of the remedies are given by Paul in our text, remedies not to be taken once, but always, remedies not just to get well, but to help us stay well. Let's take a walk through Paul's spiritual pharmacy to see which remedies might be of most help.

I.

The first item in Paul's spiritual pharmacy is labeled "rejoice," and again I say, "rejoice."

At first glance this seems a rather odd prescription from Paul, especially for his circumstances. For one thing, when he and Silas first went to Philippi years earlier, they were thrown into prison for exorcising the demons of a slave girl. Hardly a joyful situation. And now, as Paul writes this famous letter to the Philippians, one of his last, he is in prison in Rome, soon to meet his death at the hands of the Emperor Nero.

But the key to effectiveness of this medication is the added phrase, "The Lord is at hand." Paul was confident that whatever happened he was in the hands of God. He had moved beyond despair and depression to the joyful confidence that all life was a gift, especially the new life in Christ. As the Psalm advises, "Look to God and be radiant, and your faces will never be ashamed" (34:5).

II.

Another remedy in the spiritual pharmacy is labeled "forbearance."

The word forbearance means to refrain from what you have a legal right to do. It suggests fair-mindedness, a willingness to give and take, a readiness not to seek revenge, a willingness to forgive.

Recently, a professor friend of mine was giving a lively seminar to an enthusiastic audience in a church on the subject of capital punishment. He had named the pros and cons and admitted he sometimes leaned toward supporting capital punishment, though most of the time he was against it.

During the discussion period a man asked if he might speak. He stood up, and with emotion-packed voice said, "I would like to say a word about this matter of revenge and vengeance. Three years ago," he continued, "I was on the Long Island Railroad train to Garden City, New York, when the infamous massacre occurred — the one where several were killed and others were wounded."

A hush came over the seminar room as he continued. "Yes, I was one of the wounded — wounded quite badly. And for a long time I had nothing but seething anger and hatred for that despicable murderer. In fact, I had so much anger, so much hostility, so much lust for revenge, that it began to eat up my insides."

He paused as people leaned expectantly forward to hear his dramatic words. He said, "I finally realized that with all this anger and hatred I was sinking to the level of my would-be assassin. My longing for vengeance was making me almost as much a murderer as he was. And then, and then, I let it go. I decided he should not bring me down to his level, but that I should leave vengeance to someone else. Let the justice system take care of it. And I have gained great peace and contentment and strength ever since." Paul doesn't say murderers should go unpunished, but he does advise large doses of forbearance and forgiveness on the personal level.

III.

One of the more persistent maladies of the soul is anxiety. The Greek word for anxiety suggests a taffy-pull, the inward parts of our being being stretched and twisted and pounded over the cold marble of harsh reality. And at the heart of our anxiety is the sense of meaninglessness, and at the heart of meaninglessness is our awareness of death.

Popular psychoanalyst and author Rollo May says in his book *Love and Will* that "the anxiety of death — prototypically the source of all anxiety — still remains" (p. 301). And Rollo May's famous teacher at Union Theological Seminary, Dr. Paul Tillich, said in his book *The Courage to Be* that "the fear of death determines the element of anxiety ... It is the anxiety of not being able to preserve one's own being which underlies every fear ..." (p. 38).

What then shall we do in our fear of failure, our fear of meaninglessness, our fear of nothingness? Should we escape into a frenzy of moneymaking or power grabbing or pleasure seeking? Should we console ourselves in frantic fanaticisms whether they be political or religious? Should we descend into the depths of self-pity and despair and conclude with the writer of Ecclesiastes that all is vanity, that nothing makes sense?

Not that, says Paul, as he leads us through his spiritual pharmacy. Instead, he hands us a remedy labeled *"prayer."* Underneath the label it says, "Have no anxiety about anything, but in everything by prayer and supplication with thanksgiving let your requests be made known to God." And the results? "The peace of God which passes all understanding, will keep your hearts and your minds in Christ Jesus," says Paul (4:6).

Lest we immediately conjure pious, but boring, images of someone kneeling with naïve eyes steadfastly toward heaven, let us think again. Paul knew too much about the extremes of life to give glib advice on how to meet life's direst threats. He five times received the 39 lashes of the cat of nine tails, three times he was beaten with rods, and once stoned and left for dead. He was shipwrecked three times, threatened by mobs in Ephesus and other cities. He was in jail frequently and in peril often.

In Paul we have no glib, protected religious idealist handing down superficial, unreal advice. Instead, let your whole life be an attitude of prayer. Live as though you are always living in the presence of God, because you are. "The truth of Paul's gospel was not dependent on Paul," says his namesake, Paul Tillich. "Looking at God," says Tillich, "we realize all the shortcomings of our experience are of no importance. Looking at God, we see that we do not have him as an object of our knowledge, but that He has us as the subject of existence" (*The New Being*, p. 77).

And that's what prayer is — looking at God and God looking at us; living in God and God living in us. Take lots of prayer as a remedy for anxiety.

IV.

Medications for the body are innumerable and complex, ranging far beyond the chicken soup of our mothers in our childhood. The complexity and antiquity of body medications was made vivid in our recent visit to China.

As a part of our tour we visited the medical hospital in Guilin to hear a lecture on Chinese medicine, where the doctors combined modern, western medical practices with the practices and medicines of Chinese antiquity.

However, as we approached the lecture room we passed before shelves of medicines plainly visible and labeled. The one that caught my eye was a large glass jar with an amber-colored fluid labeled "Three Snake Wine." And yes, there were three, different, rather large snakes inside, dead of course, which I thought I would be if I ever drank that potion. (I hate snakes!) It was supposed to be a cure for rheumatism. I decided that if it was a choice between rheumatism and drinking Three Snake Wine, I would take the rheumatism!

If remedies for ailments of the body are complex and sometimes repulsive, Paul's remedies for the soul have an attractive and profound simplicity to them. And as we proceed in his spiritual pharmacy we come upon a remedy labeled, "*spiritual multivitamins*." And the instructions are very plain. We are to think about them, set our minds upon them, because Paul knew with the sages of old that as a person thinks in his or her heart, this is what he or she eventually becomes.

The first ingredient in this spiritual multivitamin is *truth*. We are to think actively about what is true. Stay away from the deceptive, the illusory, and the unreliable. Be careful not to be entranced with the fantasy world of Hollywood or the dream world of celebrities and sports heroes. Fame is not the same thing as immortality. Focus on the eternal truths revealed by God through his prophets and apostles and especially through his Son, Jesus the Christ.

Another multivitamin ingredient is *justice*. We seem to have a fascination with injustice and crime and violence. How else do we explain the popularity of violence in movies and television, of the *Godfather* movies which have extortion, murder, and mayhem at their core? But such a fascination only leads to a sick society. But so does despair over a criminal justice system, and even more deeply, despair over whether there is ever any true justice. Nevertheless, focus your mind on what is just, because God will bring ultimate justice, says Paul. It *is* a moral universe, because God cares. Don't despair.

Loveliness is another multivitamin ingredient — an ingredient which staves off indifference and bitterness. Helice Bridges tells a story in Canfield and Hansen's delightful book, *Chicken Soup for the Soul*, of an executive coming home to his fourteen-year-old son.

He sat his son down and said, "The most incredible thing happened to me today ... One of the junior executives came in and told me he admired me and gave me a blue ribbon for being a creative genius ... Then he put this blue ribbon that says, *Who I Am Makes A Difference* on my jacket above my heart. He gave me an extra ribbon to honor someone else."

The man continued. "As I was driving home I began to think of you. I realized I don't pay enough attention to you. I sometimes scream at you for not getting better grades, or about your bedroom being a mess. But tonight I want to tell you that you make all the difference to me, and that besides your mother, you are the most important person in my life. You're a great kid, and I love you."

His son was startled and began to sob and sob. He couldn't stop crying. His whole body shook. And through his tears he said, "I was planning on committing suicide tomorrow, Dad, because I didn't think you loved me. Now I don't need to."

Lastly, this spiritual multivitamin has an ingredient called *grace*. Think on whatever is gracious, because grace means free gift, undeserved favor, overflowing blessings which cannot be achieved but only received. And sometimes the most grace comes from unexpected places, even from children.

Dan Millman tells of his experience in Stanford Hospital as a volunteer. He got to know a little girl named Liza who was suffering from a rare and serious disease. Her only chance of recovery appeared to be a blood transfusion from her five-year-old brother, who had miraculously survived the rare disease and had developed the antibodies needed to combat the illness.

The doctor talked with the little boy, explaining the situation as best he could, and then asked the little five-year-old boy if he would be willing to give his blood to his sister. Mr. Millman says he saw the boy hesitate only a moment before taking a deep breath and saying, "Yes, I'll do it, if it will save Liza."

As the transfusion progressed he lay in bed next to his sister and smiled, as did all those present, as color began to return to Liza's cheeks. Then the little boy's face grew pale and his smile faded. He looked up at the doctor and in a trembling voice said, "Will I start to die right away?" He had misunderstood. He thought he was going to have to give her *all* his blood (*Chicken Soup for the Soul*, p. 27). Is there grace in the world? Oh, yes there is; from children, from parents, from friends and especially through Jesus, who gave all his blood, his life, for us all.

"The human mind," says Dr. William Barclay, "will always set itself on something." So think strongly about these spiritual multivitamins. They are an antidote for many spiritual diseases.

The rabbi was right. Jewish mothers knew chicken soup was a good remedy. So did my mother. And he knew that for many Jewish mothers food was love and love was food. And my mother knew that. But Paul knew greater remedies than those — remedies for the soul, spiritual remedies from a pharmacy inspired by God himself. If taken regularly and faithfully, we will enjoy robust spiritual health.

And at the bottom of all the labels Paul adds these words: "I can do all things through Christ who strengthens me."

Prayer

O Eternal God, who over the long eons of time has developed the universe and the earth, and who in the complexities of your creative processes has designed us to image you, we give you thanks and praise. With bone and marrow, flesh and blood, enzyme and hormone, DNA and RNA, you structure not only our body, but the home of our mind and soul. We are fearfully and marvelously made, overtaken in wonder and awe at the birth of each newborn baby. We adore you, O God.

Nevertheless, we bring before you today our perplexity and sometimes despair over the evil and illness in the world. There are times when disease strikes so relentlessly, so unforgivingly, so tragically. In our advanced years we have come to expect aches and ailments and the great susceptibility to life-threatening maladies. But among the young, among the innocent, disease also takes its deadly toll, and perpetually we ask, why? Why me? Why my wife? My husband, my child? O God, be attendant to our plaint and answer these perplexities of mind and heart.

Yet, we know you have not left us without hope. Within the body itself the power of healing is always at work to fight alien bacteria and viruses and to make it whole from lacerations and lesions. And within the mind and soul you have made available marvelous powers to make us whole. We thank you.

So we raise our earnest prayers for those in anguish, body or soul — for those struggling in hospitals and rehabilitation centers, for those in psychiatric wards and twelve step groups, for those carrying within their being a quiet desperation and pervasive depression. O God, see how many of us need the power of your healing touch. Come to us, heal us, make us well and whole.

And for the soul sickness of humankind which leads to war and famine, bloodshed and starvation, poverty and plague, we pray release. Let peace come to all areas troubled with evil and violence. Bring wholeness and peace. Let it be so, loving Father, and let it begin with us. Through Jesus Christ our Lord. Amen.

23. The Yeast Of The Pharisees And Herod

And he cautioned them, saying, "Take heed, beware of the leaven of the Pharisees and the leaven of Herod." — Mark 8:15

Mary Frances Fisher, feisty author of several books on food and cooking, was interviewed some time ago in her home in Glen Ellen, California. Many chefs today are more concerned about how food looks than how it tastes, she complained. Known for her forthright opinions, she was asked why she did not write a book on the classic themes of love and war. I like to write on food and drink because "there is a communion of more than our bodies when bread is broken and wine is drunk" (*Time*, January 27, 1987, p. 67).

We Christians would agree. Speak of bread and wine and we think of amber fields of waving grain and hillside vineyards glowing in California's golden sun. Speak of food and drink, and we think of earth's bounty and beauty, its fecundity beyond measure, and its productive resilience beyond imagination — signs of God's continuing grace.

It was not by accident Jesus instituted a memorial feast for his people. What better way to draw us together, as in family reunions, to remember who he was and who we are. What more basic physical survival act is there than eating and drinking, and what better act of spiritual survival can there be than that of sharing together physical bread and wine to point us to our eternal spiritual food. Mary Frances Fisher was right. When we speak of eating and drinking together there is more going on than bread and wine.

So it was in this incident in Jesus' life as reported by our text. If Jesus' disciples were worried that they had forgotten enough bread for lunch, he reminded them at once of God's providence in the feeding of the 5,000 and the 4,000. If they were preoccupied with their bellies, he reminded them of their souls. God will provide for their physical needs. They should move on to be concerned about nourishment for their souls.

In that context he warned against the yeast or leaven of Herod and the Pharisees. Powerful and pervasive, Jesus sometimes used yeast as a metaphor for the influence of the gospel in the world, which would transform a stale, flat, dull life into wholeness and vitality. But here, he uses yeast as a metaphor for the pervasive power of evil. Be wary of the yeasty, evil influences of the Pharisees and Herod. The true bread of life is not to be found with them.

I.

Consider the yeast of the Pharisees.

While many of the Pharisees were indeed wonderful, sincere, devoutly religious people, Jesus often pointed out how many other Pharisees had perverted the faith. In popular parlance, "Pharisee" became synonymous with hypocrite or phony. Externally they looked wonderfully religious like whited sepulchers, but internally they were dead and decaying. They were great on religious show and pretense, but miserly when it came to the greater issues of love and mercy and grace.

In the name of religion they exploited widows and in prideful arrogance clamored for the important seats at banquets and dinner parties. Concerned to impose the minutest, most burdensome detail of legalism on their followers, they would not, said Jesus, lift a finger to bear the burdens of others. Defensive, self-righteous, and rigidly legalistic, they had learned to exploit others in the name of religion.

The pervasive yeast of the Pharisees is very much with us today. And, yes, of course, most churches have their share of hypocrites and phonies, people who join from a variety of motives, people who make a pretense of religion but deny its real power in their lives. And, yes, of course, we still have people give us the tired, old excuse that they don't join a church because the people there aren't perfect, as if the people who don't join are perfect. The church is, as the saying goes, a hospital for sinners, not a museum for saints. Phoniness, legalism, hypocrisy, and exploitation are everywhere

— even in the churches. We should confess that and do. We would make no claim to perfection.

But think of the exploitation and phoniness and misrepresentation in the larger society — especially in the service industry. *Time* magazine (February 1, 1987) had a cover story on the shoddiness of service in our land. Our "can-do" society has become a "will-not-do" society. How many horror stories can you think of where you have been badly served — businesses promising everything but doing nothing? Have you, like me, taken your new car back three or four times to have the same thing fixed with an argument each time with a dealership which claims to pride itself on service?

Do you ever wonder what happened to the railroads? Some time ago we took the train from New York to Michigan. We had dinner in what was called, in grand exaggeration, the dining car. After the main course we could not find the waiter for dessert. Finally we found him, eating his dinner. "We are ready for dessert," we told him. "I'm eating now," he said. "Maybe I'll serve you when I'm finished!"

We are told repeatedly that ours is a service economy. In fact, 76 million workers belong to the service sector, 25 million are in goods-producing jobs, and three million are in agriculture. But rudeness, brusqueness, falsification, misrepresentation, delays, avoidance, impersonalism, and incompetence are standard characteristics. All of us know the frustration of trying to communicate with some corporation's computer which is smart, but not smart enough. A Kroger store in Morrow, Georgia, now has people check out their own groceries. In another store a customer asked the clerk, "Where's the thank you?" "It's printed on the receipt," was the reply.

This irresponsible, impersonal, exploitative yeast of the phony Pharisees is pervading our society. It's time we heed Jesus' warnings and demand truth, honesty, personal courtesy, attention, and responsible integrity.

II.

If the yeast of the Pharisees is bad, so is the yeast of Herod.

Herod was the puppet king of Israel at the time Jesus was born. Although part Jewish, he had collaborated with the Romans to maintain his position of power and wealth. He looked with disdain on the religious types who insisted on the values of the spiritual, moral life. A cynic of the first rank, he had reduced life to the question of money and power. For him, life had little meaning more than that. Talk of spiritual bread and wine if you wish, Jesus. But for Herod the real "bread" was money and power.

The issue is ever old, ever new. We regularly speak of buying and selling one another and we gladly assign a dollar value to human life. Pastoral search committees sometimes speak of buying a minister. Skeptical and cynical and financially overextended, it is easy to see life only through dollar signs.

Most alarming in recent years is the way our political system and politicians seem to be completely controlled by money more than principle. Of course we all know it takes money to run a political campaign, but do we have authentic candidates as packaged by media and public relations experts? Can we find statesmen of integrity who are not for sale? Are our politicians only looking for a parade to get in front of?

Eric Severeid once lamented in an interview that we are preoccupied with politicians who are more celebrities than statesmen. Says Severeid, think of the money politicians and ex-politicians make off their revelations, autobiographies, and memoirs. General George C. Marshall of World War II and Marshall Plan fame was asked if he would write his story for a large fee. He modestly refused, saying history would have to tell his story. Can you imagine, said Eric Severeid, Henry Kissinger doing that, or Al Haig?

In contrast to some politicians, Jimmy Carter is building houses with Habitat For Humanity in slums and ghettos. And when Harry Truman declined lucrative offers after leaving the White House, he said: "I could never lend myself to any transaction, however respectable, that would commercialize on the prestige and dignity of the office of the Presidency." His advice no doubt seems quaint now as Presidents and astronauts make big money off what we gave them. It's the yeast of Herod, isn't it?

It is for us to gather around the table of true bread and wine for the yeast of the gospel, the pervasive influence of our Lord Jesus Christ. We gather to be nourished against phoniness and exploitation. We gather to be reminded that we cannot serve God *and* mammon, for we will either love mammon and use God, or love God and use mammon, as we ought. We gather for the gracious spiritual nourishment which leads to integrity, honesty, faithful service, and life eternal.

Prayer

Loving Father, who appears to have created the world across the aeons of time with a certain wild profligacy, but who in recent times has focused yourself in Jesus Christ to recreate a world gone awry, praise be to you for making us a part of your grand scheme of things entire and for bearing patiently with us as we learn and re-learn your design. We thank you for all we are and all we can become.

Look upon us with mercy as we acknowledge our faltering faith and erratic discipleship. We are pulled this way and that by force and counter force, opinion and opposite opinion. Unsure of our own convictions, we are swayed too much by the convictions of others. Beset ourselves with doubts we yield too readily to the uncertain certainties of others. Following Jesus more and more from a distance, we are too ready, like Peter, to deny him while we warm ourselves by the enemy's fire. Forgive our fickle faith and wavering loyalty.

As we gather around your table, refresh us with your spiritual food. If we have become weary in well-doing, release us from the burden of self-righteousness to relax into your grace. If we have become cynical in our failures, help us to be encouraged by your promises of overcoming that which would defeat us. If we have lost faith in you only to place it in a lesser God or cause, give us insight to see our folly and help us to cleanse our hearts of all duplicity.

We pray for the Church, that it might grow from strength to strength nourished by your Word and by your bread and wine. And for the world, we ask wholeness, justice, and peace. In Christ's name we pray. Amen.

24. A Spiritual Bouquet For A Spiritual Banquet

The fruit of the spirit is love, joy, peace, patience, kindness, goodness, faithfulness, gentleness, self-control; against such there is no law.
— Galatians 5:22-23

Some years ago, Hulda Niebuhr, sister of the famous Niebuhr brothers, Reinhold and Richard, wrote a book about Jesus titled *Greatness Passing By*. I have always liked that title because throughout history, great men and women, like Jesus, have been passing by and so many people did not recognize them.

The same is true for ideas. The prophets Amos and Jeremiah were scorned by secular and religious leaders alike for their progressive ideas. Socrates was condemned by his fellow citizens. Paul was stoned and left for dead by religious conservatives incensed with his liberal ideas. Soren Kierkegaard, the now famous Danish philosopher and theologian, was largely ignored in Denmark in the early 1800s. He predicted his ideas would not be appreciated until fifty years from his death — a prediction that came true to make him one of the most influential thinkers of the twentieth century.

If great ideas pass by unnoticed, so do great artists. A woman was visiting the Metropolitan Museum of Art in New York City and said to her friend while gazing at an artistic masterpiece, "In my judgment, I don't see what is so great about the painting." The museum guard, overhearing her, could not resist saying to her, "Madam, if you will pardon me for saying so, I think that more than you judging the painting, the painting is judging you."

So it was with the now-famous artist Vincent Van Gogh. Unappreciated in his own time when he sold not a single painting, now his paintings seem to judge all would-be critics by being sold for millions of dollars. Greatness passed by, and it took years for greatness to become recognized.

Such was the case with Van Gogh's paintings of bouquets of flowers. His still life of flowers, his flowers in a blue vase, his oleanders and irises, all from the late 1880s, waited for recognition and high prices. And so did his famous bouquet of sunflowers to which we would draw attention today. For it is the apt symbol of the spiritual bouquet essential for a spiritual banquet.

And the irony is that Van Gogh's own life and work are symbolic of two contrasting bouquets — the one self-destructive, the other life-giving.

I.

Consider first *the destructive bouquet of Van Gogh's own life, the bouquet of death.*

Born in 1853 in the Netherlands to a Dutch Reformed pastor and his wife, Van Gogh was a highly sensitive and brilliant man. Although from a family of pastors, he had two uncles who were art dealers who made important art connections for him in London and Paris.

But before art, Van Gogh was rebuffed two or three times in love and later rebuffed in his efforts to be a minister. He went to work among the poor in Belgium, "abased himself to their level of destitution, slept on a board in a wooden hut, shared their privations, cared for the sick, and displayed all the inspired zeal of an apostle" (*Van Gogh*, by Frank Elgar, p. 2). But his zeal and intensity appeared more as madness than devotion and compassion, so they rejected him.

Van Gogh took up with an ugly, drunken prostitute, then mourned his father's death, received support from his brother, Theo, so he could go to Paris to paint. And paint he did, in a kind of frenzy, creating many of his greatest works the last years of his life in an insane asylum. But not before in a fit of rage and guilt he cut off his ear and gave it to a prostitute in a brothel. And then, tragically, as we know, he ended his life by shooting himself in a manure pile, dying two days later with his brother, Theo, at his side.

Vincent Van Gogh had terrible and tragic and destructive forces at work within him, which though utilized to produce magnificent art, eventually brought the bouquet of his life to ruin.

As with Van Gogh, so with the Church, the very art we produce, the very words and ethics, literature and teachings, music and art came to flourish while the Church itself becomes self-destructive. As with Van Gogh, so also in the Church, passions and forces out of control can cause the Church to decay, even to take its own life in a manure pile.

What are some of those forces that produce the deadly, destructive, fleshly bouquet? Paul names them — forces which conflict with life and health, beauty and balance, and lead eventually to death. The forces are fleshly desires, from the Greek word, *epithemion*, which means passions and angers and hostilities which flame up suddenly like ignited gasoline.

One destructive force was that of fornication, which included not only prostitution, but all sexual vice and immorality and unfaithfulness to marriage vows.

Another suicidal force was that of lasciviousness and licentiousness, which suggest unrestrained violence and willfulness, doing what we please without regard for anyone else.

Forces of idolatry, that is, the impulse to worship what we have made, whether it be a statue, a state, or a system of thought, can be destructive. Witchcraft and sorcery, with their attendant use of drugs and magic in an attempt to force God to do our will rather than vice versa, will wither the bouquet of life at its core.

Or think of hatred, enmity, rivalry, strife, discord, quarrels, derision, distraction, division, jealousies, flashes of uncontrolled anger, seditions and dissensions, and the damage they can do to the flower of life.

The partisan spirit is especially destructive, because in an age of individualism it always thinks its ideas are right, charging forward with self-righteous opinions, without ever asking what Christ's opinion might be.

If you want to wilt a bouquet and destroy the bouquet of family or Church, just let these forces get going and they will lead to madness, mutual destruction, and suicide. Vincent Van Gogh was an extremely sensitive and gifted genius, but there were forces at work within him, probably beyond his control, which brought him to suicide.

So too with humankind, so often gifted and sensitive with geniuses everywhere. Unless these destructive forces are brought under control, the flowering of all humanity will end in a heap beside a pile of manure.

II.

If that is the fleshly bouquet of death, consider now *the spiritual bouquet of life.*

If we lament the tragic personal life of Van Gogh, we celebrate the artistic side, because there he brought forth a beautiful spiritual bouquet, to bless the world and give it life. In his own time, he was greatness passing by, and very few people knew it. But in our time, his greatness has come into its own.

So also with Jesus and his Church. In his own time, Jesus was greatness passing by, and few people knew it. But in these twenty centuries, his greatness has come into its own with millions and millions of people. Like his latter-day disciple, Soren Kierkegaard, whose ideas were scorned during his life, after his death they were revered and became a beautiful psychological, philosophical, and theological bouquet for the world; so too Jesus' ideas, once scorned, have produced life-giving, beautiful, spiritual bouquets for centuries.

And if we were to paint a bouquet and place flowers in a vase like a spiritual Van Gogh, what would we put there? We would, says Paul, following in the footsteps of Jesus, put the everlastingly beautiful long-stemmed flower of love. This would not be just a selfish love, but a self-giving love, a love thoughtful of others and their needs as well as of its own needs.

Another important blossom of the Holy Spirit we would add would be that of joy, not a forced joy, but a deep internal happiness or blessed-ness which comes from the graciousness of God. And then we would add the all-important blossom of peace, *eirene* or *shalom*, that deep inward sense of well-being and balance and serenity, that peace which passes all understanding, because it infuses us with the assurance that we are accepted by God, that we need not be anxious about our inadequate backgrounds.

Another blossom in our spiritual bouquet to grace our spiritual banquet table would be that of long-suffering or patience. The root word here suggests someone who is able to control for a long time the *themia*, the sudden passions which tend to flame up inside us to consume us and others.

Kindness is then added to our bouquet to overcome the tendency toward unkindness. Its sister blossoms are courtesy, gentleness, thoughtfulness, generosity, considerateness. In a world of pushy aggressiveness and abrasive selfishness, what a refreshing thing it is to come upon a bouquet of kindly flowers lending their beauty and fragrance to all around them, blessing them, calming them, helping them, healing them. Add to that the blossom of self-control, of self-mastery, and we have a beautiful bouquet indeed.

Were these ideas ahead of their time? Were they greatness passing by? Yes. They always are ahead of the times. Were the Galatian Christians having problems with quarrels and divisions and dissensions? Were some of them trying to destroy the others, even their ministers and Paul the Apostle?

Indeed they were, but eventually they and all the Church saw these ideas as greatness passing by. It is possible, said Paul, to bite and devour one another like wild animals following their base instincts for survival and territory. But it is also possible to build one another up in love, to make a beautiful spiritual bouquet, not only for our spiritual banquet but also for the community and the world.

And that brings us back to Vincent Van Gogh and one of his famous paintings of sunflowers in a vase. When you look at the individual sunflowers, they are not, by themselves, all that beautiful. Some are a little disfigured, others are a little wilted and droopy.

And yet together, they are a beautiful sight, holding one another up to be a beautiful bouquet of the soul. So too, the Church, composed of each of us as individual sunflowers, each a little bit imperfect here and there, some a little wilted and faded and droopy, and yet together, holding each other up, bearing one another's burdens, we can become a beautiful spiritual bouquet worthy of a Van Gogh, or even of the master human artist himself, Jesus Christ.

And such is the spiritual bouquet Christ would have with him at his spiritual banquet.

Prayer

Almighty God, whose loving power generates a multiplicity of life in a sometimes forbidding universe, and whose creative impulse causes seed to bring forth after its own kind, to bless the earth with beauty and bounty, we praise and adore you for your providential care. With beauty and splendor beyond our telling, you entrance the eye, and with subtlety and variety beyond description you satisfy tongue and taste to nourish and sustain us. We give thanks, O God.

Ages ago, in geological time, you brought forth flowers upon the earth, in an instant, as it were — flowers hardy and delicate, large and small, intricate and plain. From mountainside edelweiss to jungle orchid, from temperate rose to torrid lilies, from rain forest lushness to desert cactus flowers, you make all the world to bloom with the multiplicity of your splendor. We praise you.

As with flowers, so with us. It has pleased you to create us male and female, in varieties of sizes and shapes, races and colorings, languages and physiques. You delight yourself in our distinctive diversities, giving us each special gifts to bless the Church and world.

Help us then, O Lord, to bring to full flower the gift you have given us. If ours is the gift of intelligence, then let us use it with the humility befitting those aware of how little they know. If ours is the gift of feeling and compassion, help us use it without condescension. If we can make music better than most, may it be music drawing hearts and minds to you and one another.

If we have a way with words, let us never be wordy, but rather worthy of expressing great thought and feeling. If ours is the gift of money-making, turning to gold almost everything we touch, save us from greed, and lead us to generosity to create jobs for others and to help those in need. If ours is the gift of a strong will, let it never degenerate into stubbornness, but be used to strengthen the spirit of others. If we can see the bright side and maintain hope in the darkest of days, grant us strength to encourage others with sympathy.

If ours is the gift of artistic expression, or cooking, or administration, or cleaning, or organization, or designing, or building, or planning, or writing, or teaching — whatever our gift, help us, O Lord, to bring it to full flower to bless ourselves, the Church, and all the world with a spiritual bouquet, fragrant and beautiful. In Christ's name we pray. Amen.

25. Table Manners In A Hungry World

And at his gate lay a poor man named Lazarus, full of sores, who desired to be fed with what fell from the rich man's table; moreover the dogs came and licked his sores. — Luke 16:20-21

The opening scene in the popular movie, *Trading Places*, shows the lead character as a black beggar on a Philadelphia sidewalk. Sitting on a low, square board with four castors on the bottom, the lead character pushes his way along, begging for alms. As a blind paraplegic clothed in a Vietnam veteran's uniform, he is able to play on people's sympathies for generous contributions.

However, two tough Philadelphia policemen are not as sympathetic. Following up reports on the blind paraplegic, they move in, lift him from his skateboard-type cart, and work him over. After some delightful bluffing, the lead character finally opens his eyes and stands up in excellent physical health. He is promptly arrested.

But that is only the beginning of the story. Two wealthy, eccentric businessmen learn of him, bail him out, and offer him a high position in their business. All this is done on a bet that environment largely determines a man's destiny.

At the same time, these two eccentric businessmen-brothers cause their carefully groomed, well-educated, white, young executive to be discredited. Soon he is out of a job, out of money, out of his house with butler and car with chauffeur and out of friends — except for a prostitute who takes pity on him.

So far the experiment seems to be working. The black beggar, in his new environment, rises to the occasion, becomes protective of his property, critical of his former friends, and wise and successful in the business. In contrast, the well-groomed, white, young executive, is now destitute, driven to petty thievery to survive, to boorishness and grubbiness. Environment and opportunity do seem to make the man. They have traded places — one from poverty to riches, the other from riches to poverty.

Farcical and preposterous at times, the movie is good for a lot of laughs. And it has some similarity to our text where Lazarus and Dives trade places. One goes from poverty and suffering to eternal bliss; the other from earthly wealth and comfort to eternal deprivation and punishment. Like the movie, it is a story of the great reversal, of trading places.

Though the movie tends to be farcical, Jesus' parable is more serious. Not without its humor and irony, Jesus' story has an abiding and haunting relevance. And like the movie, the story is a drama, highly condensed and powerful.

I.

In act one we have the two principle players, Dives which means "rich," and Lazarus which means "one whom God has helped."

Dives is exceedingly wealthy. Clothed in the finest purples and linens, he dines on the best of foods *every* day. Servants attend to his every need and whim. He obviously is enjoying the ultimate in the good life.

No doubt Dives was a member of the Sadducean party, which consisted largely of wealthy, aristocratic landholders. From their group came also the priests of the Jerusalem Temple who succeeded to those positions only by heredity. Between them, the priests and landholders had a near monopoly on money, power, and social position in the time of Jesus.

The Sadducees believed only the first five books of the Bible to be inspired and therefore authoritative for life. They adhered strongly to the Deuteronomic theology which had been popularized to say that if you were righteous, you would be blessed with good fortune. If you were unrighteous you would have misfortune. Further, the Sadducees believed in no after-life, except possibly a shadowy, half-conscious existence in Sheol, the pit of death.

Therefore, in the popular Sadducean theology of the time, Dives was the shining example of the righteous. It was obvious he was righteous, because God had blessed him with wealth, power, and social position. Since there was for Sadducees no life after death, he was thought to be receiving the greatest of God's rewards for human life. He was envied in the city. The poor and middle classes gladly would have traded places with him, but they assumed they must be somehow unrighteous and unworthy.

Perhaps that was the thought of Lazarus, the poor beggar who sat at Dives' door waiting for scraps of garbage. We are not told why Lazarus was a beggar. Possibly the boils all over his body were evidence of some sort of disease which made him unemployable. Clothed in rags, he competed with the stray dogs for the bits of bread thrown out the back door. Far from bakery delicacies, these pieces of bread were used by guests to wipe food and grease from their hands and then were thrown under the table to be gathered by servants to be thrown into the street.

In the popular theology of the day, Lazarus was the perfect example of the unrighteous man, cursed by God. Obviously he had sinned in some serious way because he was destitute and covered with boils. Perhaps he had once been like the proverbial Job who lost fortune and family and became covered with boils because, as his friends said, he had committed some grievous sin. At any rate, it was clear to Dives and all his Sadducean friends, that Lazarus was a man to avoid because he was an obvious sinner, avoided by God and cursed by God.

It is interesting to note that the Deuteronomic theology is alive and well today. Many well-to-do, well-connected people believe they have been blessed by God because of their right thinking and right acting. At the same time they often believe the poor are poor because they deserve it. And sometimes the poor think in similar ways.

But today, as in Jesus' time, often wealth and poverty, health and disease are products of birth and chance. Some of us are born into wealth and privilege and connections without ever working to achieve them on our own. Others of us are born into poverty and anonymity and destitution without ever having done anything to deserve them. To a considerable extent, we are products of environment, heredity, and chance.

II.

In the second scene in this tiny, poignant drama, heaven and hell are on one small stage.

Both Dives and Lazarus have died and their roles are exactly reversed. Now Lazarus is relieved of his starvation and suffering, made whole and complete in heaven, resting at the bosom of Abraham. Once begging for a piece of bread at Dives' gate, Lazarus now enjoys the fullness of the life of Paradise.

But Dives is now in hell, begging Abraham to send Lazarus to touch his tongue with cool water to relieve the torment of the flames. Dives apparently has not changed much. He still thinks of Lazarus as a beggar and servant, asking him to be sent to serve him with water. But the time of penitence has passed. Dives has had his joy on earth, and Lazarus his misery. But now in Jesus' ironical story, the Deuteronomic theology is contradicted and the roles are reversed. Dives, who believed in no judgment or after-life, is subject to both. And once believing himself fully blessed by God, he now finds himself cursed. Once content he was a true Son of Abraham by genetic pedigree, he now sees the despised Lazarus, who is without pedigree, at Abraham's bosom.

However, it is important to note that Dives is not condemned for his wealth as such, nor is Lazarus praised for his poverty. Jesus' classic story should not be misconstrued to have him praising failure and poverty and cursing success and wealth. Jesus does not teach that the poor are automatically virtuous and that the rich are automatically wicked. His story is not an endorsement of begging and a condemnation of business and moneymaking.

Among some socialists and liberation theologians of today, there seems to be a reversal of the Deuteronomic theology. Whereas the Deuteronomic theologians said wealth was a sign of righteousness and God's blessing, some socialists and liberation theologians of today seem to say that wealth is a sign of wickedness and unrighteousness. Some go so far as to say that behind every profit is a major crime.

At the Fosdick Convocation On Preaching in New York City, one of the Latin American liberation theologians contributed to the ambiguity of many present-day Christians. In the first part of his speech he was highly condemnatory of Western materialism and especially of American wealth. He reminded us of Jesus' teachings about money and his warnings about the dangers of riches. We got the impression that he expected us to divest ourselves of all our possessions for the sake of entering the Kingdom. It was as if he were Lazarus preaching at the gate of an American Dives, condemning him for his wealth.

But in the latter part of his speech, the South American theologian shifted gears saying how important it was for the third world countries to share in the world's wealth. In his inaccurate theology he seemed to condemn wealth and material on the one hand, but on the other he wanted to make sure his people got their share, and plenty of it.

So it is that many well-meaning theologians and socialists confuse their thinking. Instead of condemning wealth and success, they are more accurate to press their rightful claims for sharing. Instead of railing against the West for being successful, they would be better to encourage the West to share know-how and investments so that third world countries could indeed enjoy their rightful share of the world's abundance.

This story of Jesus is not a call for simple-minded and sentimental sharing with the poor. After all, Dives did at least throw out his scraps to Lazarus, much as we give a dollar to a beggar to get him off our backs, or ten dollars to relief agency to relieve our guilt feelings for having such a good life while so many are hungry and poor.

While this story is designed to promote personal charity through sharing food and clothing, medicine and money, with the needy, it really is not license for a simple-minded, give-away program. That surely will not relieve the hunger pangs of the world. Remember when the captors of Patti Hearst demanded the Hearst family give away millions of dollars worth of food to the poor in San Francisco? It lasted a few days and was gone. Indeed, in a few more days the whole Hearst fortune would have been given away with no long-lasting alleviation of poverty or hunger. The fortunes of the world's wealthiest people would not last long in an outright giveaway. Obviously, in a hungry world Christian concepts of charity and sharing must move beyond such simple-mindedness.

While Christians should never cease in personal charity and contributions through private agencies where they can do enormous good, they must move on to more creative and sophisticated ways of sharing. Christian executives in third-world countries can encourage progressive, rather than exploitative, wage scales. A social conscience as well as business acumen are needed in all levels of enterprise. A forthright and open concern for the suffering and disadvantaged often reaps enormous rewards for all, as in the case of the Marshall Plan for Europe after World War II. After all, a restored Europe was able to do far more business with us than a devastated Europe. Likewise with Japan. Actually, it is to everyone's enlightened self-interest to enable peoples everywhere to participate in the world economy, sharing its work and responsibility and enjoying its fruits and blessings.

Notice that Jesus does not say that Dives should support Lazarus on a perpetual welfare program. But he does imply that the privileged Dives should have gotten medical attention for Lazarus, so he could be healed, get a job, and become self-supporting. To the lazy and indolent, to the con artists and moochers and exploiters, Jesus would say with Paul, if a man won't work when he is able, don't let him eat.

Great Britain's former prime minister Margaret Thatcher once said that those who insist on a welfare state assume that someone, somewhere must be producing the wealth to pay for the welfare. Lazarus is not praised for begging. Instead, Dives is condemned for not helping Lazarus in his desperate need for healing and employment. Indeed, someone has observed that if every business in our country hired just one more person, our unemployment problems would be greatly solved. Many of us know at least one person we can help with health, food, and employment opportunities.

So on several fronts we are called upon to share with those in need in a hungry world. On the personal, the corporate, and the governmental levels we are urged to share and to help in ways that are both simple and direct as well as sophisticated and indirect. Otherwise Jesus' words may well apply to us where he says:

"Blessed are you poor, for yours is the Kingdom of God ... But woe to you that are rich, for you have received your consolation" (Luke 6:20b, 24).

III.

The last scene in this condensed drama comes unexpectedly. Dives asks that his five brothers might be warned so they can avoid the torment of hell.

We may assume that Dives' brothers were well-to-do aristocratic Sadducees like him. Although we may assume they were selfish and greedy like Dives, they undoubtedly thought themselves righteous and blessed by God. Claiming direct descent from Abraham they presumed their impeccable pedigree entitled them to the full benefits of God's Kingdom which they rightfully were enjoying here and now. Believing there was no judgment and no punishment or reward in life after death, they strove to build their paradise in this world. But from his torment in hell, Dives beseeches Abraham to send messengers to warn his family.

It is by this parable Jesus is warning all who have eyes to see and ears to hear. If we are content to build a private paradise with no concern for the poor and needy, if we have convinced ourselves there is no judgment and no after-life, if we have thought ourselves naturally righteous because we are well-off, if we have hardened our heart to the brother and sister in need because we believe they are poor because they deserve it, if we have set our hearts upon pedigree, genealogy, and riches instead of upon God — then let us be warned by this startling parable of our Lord.

No other words will be given. No other sign or portent will be shown. People will not come back from the dead to warn us. We have our warning as of now. Table manners in a hungry world call for us to share generously from our abundance with those in need. And we are to do so with wisdom, sophistication, and above all, with love.

Prayer

Eternal God, out of whose power of being all life has come, and who has designed the world to be prolific beyond measure, scattering trillions upon trillions of seeds for life to come out of life after its own kind; praise be to you for the fecundity and bounty we enjoy from your hand. The fruits of the harvest and the colors of the seasons bedazzle us with splendor and variety. The fragrances, as gentle and soft as the colors, entrance us, and the tastes of all the world's produce continue to be our delight. We celebrate the life you have given us, O God, and praise you for a world sensuous and wonderful, with stimuli splendid.

We praise you for ways in which you have blessed us. With good educational opportunities, with supportive families and good health, with friendships firm, and with affluence and abundance you have blessed many of us. We are grateful for this free land where initiative often is rewarded, this grand country where energetic enterprise often reaps a harvest of unprecedented bounty. Thanks be to you for all that has made this good life possible.

But in our prosperity and success, grant that we may not be inflated with pride or infected with arrogance. In the accumulation of this world's goods, grant that we may not gain the world and lose our souls. In the successful provision for our temporal, material needs, grant that we may even more provide for spiritual, eternal needs. If the world entrances us it can also delude us, if the abundance of goods of the material life satisfies us, remind us that it satisfies not the hunger and thirst for life eternal which you have planted within us. So we come to you, our loving Eternal Father, to set our hearts on eternal things.

Grant that in a needy world, ours may not be the cynical mind and hardened heart. Open our eyes to see the suffering and pain which we might help assuage and heal. From our gourmet tables, make us sensitive to those struggling for scraps of bread and a drink of water. Open to us new and creative ways of sharing and helping. Through Jesus Christ our Lord. Amen.

26. The Feast Of Expectation

They shall hunger no more, neither thirst any more; the sun shall not strike them, nor any scorching heat. For the Lamb in the midst of the throne will be their shepherd, and he will guide them to springs of living water; and God will wipe away every tear from their eyes. — Revelation 7:16-17

Some of my fondest memories of years past are of family reunions at holidays and anniversaries. During college years or the early years of marriage, it was fun to anticipate returning to my parents' home for family gatherings. Not the least of my expectations was the sharing of good food around the dining room table. We could count on Mom to come forth with some of her excellent dishes, of which we would eat more than we should. But we could always diet later, we told ourselves.

As time has passed and our own family has grown, the focus has shifted somewhat. If once we looked forward to Grandmother's house and good food, now our own children, thank God, look forward to returning home to us on holidays and anniversaries. For them and us, it is a time of anticipation and expectancy, not the least of which is the expectancy of my wife's excellent food. One Christmas we were fortunate to have all our children home. We had a bonus day when our out-of-towners were snowed in. So after dinner, we sat around the table for almost two hours, singing and talking. It doesn't get much better than that.

Family gatherings can be those great occasions of re-grouping and re-thinking who we are. If Robert Frost whimsically observed that home is where, when you go there, they have to take you in, most of us would jubilantly affirm home as a place where we remember who we are and from whence we came. And if in the vicissitudes and defeats of life we often feel exhausted and depressed, home and family meals can be those occasions of refreshment where love is made real and where meaning and purpose are restored.

So it is the Church is a family — the family of God and Christ. And we too have our homecomings and holidays, our festival meals and reunions. Communion is just such an occasion, especially World Communion Sunday, when Christians a billion strong go home again to remember who they are and from whence they came. It is a time of refreshment and encouragement, where the wounds of life are healed, a time for nourishment for the pilgrimage of faith, a time for recovery of purpose and meaning.

I.

But if World Communion Sunday brings us together in time and space, it also brings us together to transcend time and space, to point us to a glad triumphal reunion beyond life and death, to the marriage supper of the Lamb, to the great banquet of heaven, the wonderful homecoming of all Christ's people. Not only do we come around the temporal table in expectation of sustenance and renewal; we are there infused with a transcendent expectation for the everlasting table of God.

Lovers of good food and drink that most of us are, we do have to be reminded of the transitoriness of all our human feasting. If cookbooks sell nearly as well as Bibles, and infinitely better than books of sermons or prayers, we do need to hear again the Apostle Paul's words that the Kingdom of God does not consist of food and drink, but of righteousness and peace and joy in the Holy Spirit (Romans 14:17). Meaningful and fun as our family meals can be, they are, in a sense, a foretaste of the eternal feast of God, where we partake of the eternal bread and the water from the fountains of life.

This leads us then to the other side of family occasions — those times when the family circle is broken. As we often say, families seem only to get together for weddings and funerals. And it is only natural food and drink should be a part of the occasion to sustain us in both joy and sorrow. But in the sorrow we are made aware of the limitations of temporal food against the powers of death.

Thus, around the Communion table we are reminded not to give our ultimate labor for the food which perishes, but for the bread which gives life eternal. If in our earthly striving we long for the best feasts and the gourmet dinner parties, let the Communion arouse us to the transitoriness of the passing scene, and awaken us to the eternal banquet which the Lord is preparing for those who love him and are called according to his purpose.

II.

However, there is another side to the feast of expectancy. If it serves as a warning to those of us rich enough to enjoy the sumptuous feasts of this life, it is a sign of hope for those whose existence is from hand to mouth, for those who go to bed hungry every night, whose hunger pains never stop and for whom disease and devastation are the victors because of malnutrition.

John's Revelation was written about 96 A.D., during a time of great persecution. The Emperor Domitian demanded that Christians bow the knee to him, burn incense to him, and proclaim him as Lord. Since Christians of integrity could worship no man as Lord, they often were exiled (as was the case with John), or had their property confiscated by the state, or were imprisoned or beaten or killed. John's entire book is written to encourage Christians to keep the faith in the terrible time of crisis. Do not give up allegiance to the Eternal King for a few years of safety with a temporal king, said John. You may be devastated now, but you will be given the eternal bread and water so you will never hunger or thirst again.

And what causes world hunger for daily bread? Ignorance, to be sure. Poor agricultural methods and overpopulation contribute. But one of the main causes is corrupt political regimes which are fueled by greed and lust for power. The famine and plagues and wars of which John speaks are usually the result of oppressive, totalitarian regimes. In the lust for power, a king or dictator attacks, thousands are displaced or killed, crops are ruined, and the balance of nature is disturbed and food production is interrupted.

Consider Ethiopia. Much of their problem is related to the deforestation of the country, which in turn led to erosion of the topsoil, which in turn led to poor productivity which led to hunger. Loss of the forests also affected the ecological cycle contributing to draught which leads to famine. The trees were cut in the first place, as the result of wholesale greed, as often they were in America.

Further, Ethiopia devoted itself to cash crops such as cotton, coffee, and tobacco in place of life-sustaining wheat and barley and corn. It devoted itself to cash crops so that military leaders could have cash to buy military weaponry to keep themselves in power. Thus, thousands upon thousands starved to death because of demonic greed and lust for power.

While Holy Communion is not meant to be a feast for escaping economic and political problems, it is a feast of reassurance. For the oppressed of the earth, it is a feast of hope that someday justice will be done, that someday the poor shall inherit the Kingdom, that someday those who hunger and thirst after righteousness shall be filled.

Of course, this does not release us from works of compassion and justice in striving toward a more equitable world. But it does say that for probably the majority of the world's people, that day will not come before their death. Therefore, we share the temporal bread and wine in the expectation they shall share the eternal bread and wine in heaven's great welcome-home banquet.

So it is we go to the Communion table in expectation. If we are rich and full with this world's food and wine, we are at the table awakened to the transitoriness of wealth and power and of life itself. And if we are empty and powerless, we are assured the injustice of man will be corrected by the justice of God. All this is to say we are in the world having as having not. It is to say with Paul that we are citizens of heaven from which we expect Christ to return to transform us into spiritual glory to participate in the grand, eternal homecoming party.

Or it is to say with John, "They shall hunger no more, neither thirst anymore. The sun shall not strike them nor any scorching heat. For the Lamb in the midst of the throne will be their shepherd, and he will guide them to springs of living water; and God will wipe away every tear from their eyes" (Revelation 7:16-17). Let us eat and drink together with that expectation.

Prayer

Eternal God, who dwells in the effulgence of light unapproachable, far beyond the grasp of time and space, and yet who makes yourself known in the light of conscience and the acts of love; we creatures of time and sense worship and adore you. In our late night dreams and early morning visions, we catch glimpses of realities beyond the mundane. By the power of your Spirit through the holy scriptures, we are aroused again to faith and hope and love, made ready again for your Kingdom coming — ever coming to those ready to receive it. Thank you for pursuing us through victory and tragedy to claim us as your own.

O God, you have brought us into the world for freedom and love, but we only can confess the tragic misuse of our freedom and our frequent participation in wrong and evil. More than that, we acknowledge our submission to powerful forces seemingly beyond our control — forces of greed and lust, fear and revenge, and the craving for power and glory. So we come to you, O Lord, for inward power to choose the good and to resist evil. Infuse us with your Spirit, that we shall be able to stand faithfully in the evil day. Forgive us those times we have failed you, and create a new heart within us, we pray.

Merciful Father, loving and compassionate, who has promised to bind up the wounds of the broken-hearted, we bring to you the tears and grief of life. See what bitter disappointments often are ours. Some of us struggle with a debilitating disease that just will not let go; some of us are in constant physical pain; some of us have hearts pierced through with many sorrows; some of us are embittered within marriage and others lonely in divorce; some of us are in financial straits or have experienced financial defeat and unemployment; some of us have lost friends; some have lost loved ones to death itself; and perhaps many of us, in a sometimes cruel and evil world, have lost faith itself, and hope and love.

O Eternal God, who has sent us to school in this sometimes strange life of ours, renew us, we pray. Heal us with the balm of Gilead and lift our eyes to your larger horizon where even now a new sun is rising for a new day. In Christ's name we pray. Amen.

Bibliography

Baillie, D. M., *The Theology of the Sacraments*, New York, New York, Charles Scribner's Sons, 1957

Bates, Marston, *The Forest and the Sea*, New York, New York, Time Incorporated, 1960

Becker, Ernest, *Escape from Evil*, New York, New York, The Free Press, 1975

Becker, Ernest, *The Denial of Death*, New York, New York, The Free Press, 1973

Bloom, Allan, *The Closing of the American Mind*, New York, New York, Simon & Schuster, 1987

Boyd, Malcom, *Are You Running With Me, Jesus?* New York, New York, Avon Books, 1965

Buttrick, George, editor, *The Interpreter's Bible*, New York, New York, Abingdon Press, 1952

Canfield, Jack and Hansen, Mark Victor, *Chicken Soup for the Soul*, Deerfield Beach, Florida, Health Communications, Inc., 1993

Collis, John Stewart, *The Vision of Glory*, New York, New York, George Braziller, 1973

Dickinson, Emily, *The Complete Poems of Emily Dickinson*, edited by Thomas H. Johnson, Boston, Massachusetts, Little, Brown and Company, 1960

Dillard, Annie, *Pilgrim at Tinker Creek*, New York, New York, Bantam Books, Inc., 1974

Elgar, Frank, *Van Gogh*, Woodbury, New York, Barron's, 1981

Frost, Robert, *The Poems of Robert Frost*, New York, New York, Random House, 1946

Keck, Leander E., *The Church Confident*, Nashville, Tennessee, Abingdon Press, 1993

L'Engle, Madeleine, *Two-Part Invention*, San Francisco, California, Harper & Row Publishers, 1988

May, Rollo, *Love and Will*, New York, New York, W.W. Norton & Company, Inc., 1969

Michener, James, *Centennial*, New York, New York, Random House, 1974

Mills, C. Wright, *The Power Elite*, New York, New York, Oxford University Press, 1959

Nash, Ogden, *I Wouldn't Have Missed It*, Boston, Massachusetts, Little, Brown and Company, 1975

Niebuhr, Reinhold, *The Nature and Destiny of Man*, Vols. I and II, New York, New York, Charles Scribner's Sons, 1964

Niebuhr, Hulda, *Greatness Passing By*, New York, New York, Charles Scribner's Sons, 1931

Russell, Franklin, *Watchers at the Pond*, New York, New York, Time Incorporated, 1961

de St. Exupery, Antoine, *Wind, Sand and Stars*, New York, New York, Time Incorporated, 1965 (translated by Lewis Galantiere)

Tillich, Paul, *The Courage To Be*, New York, New York, Yale University Press, 1952

Tillich, Paul, *The New Being*, New York, New York, Charles Scribner's Sons, 1955

West, J. B., *Upstairs at the White House*, New York, New York, Coward, McCann & Geoghegan, 1973

Williams, H. A., *True Resurrection*, Springfield, Illinois, Templegate Publishers, 1972

Wolfe, Thomas, *The Bonfire of the Vanities*, New York, New York, Farrar, Straus, Giroux, 1989

Wood, Barry, *The Magnificent Frolic*, Philadelphia, Pennsylvania, The Westminster Press, 1970

www.ingramcontent.com/pod-product-compliance
Lightning Source LLC
Chambersburg PA
CBHW070737160426
43192CB00009B/1468